Advanced Grant Writing for International Funding

LEARNING OUTCOMES

UNDERSTAND THE CONCEPT OF FUNDING AND PHILANTROPY

LEARN TO THINK LIKE A FUNDER

UNDERSTAND THE GRANT LIFECYCLE

LEARN HOW BOILER PLATES WORK

UNDERSTAND THE COMPONENTS OF GRANT WRITING

LEARN HOW TO WRITE A PROFESSIONAL GRANT PROPOSAL

LEARN HOW TO SOURCE FOR DATA AND CITE SOURCES

LEARN STORY-TELLING STRATEGIES

LEARN GRANT MANAGEMENT AND REPORTING TECHNIQUES

LEARN PROFESSIONAL GRANT WRITING PRACTICES AND ETHICS

ACCESS TO PHRASE BANK

LEARN ABOUT BLACKLIST PHRASES

ACCESS TO PROFESSIONAL GRANT WRITING TOOLS

What's Inside

Grant Writing in International Development

International development encompasses a wide range of activities, including poverty alleviation, healthcare, education, infrastructure development, environmental conservation, and much more. These initiatives require funding to operate effectively and make a meaningful impact. In a globalized world, grant writing stands as a critical link connecting the resources of donors with the pressing needs of communities worldwide.

Grant writing is the primary means by which organizations in international development secure financial support for their initiatives. These organizations, including non-governmental organizations (NGOs), governmental agencies, and community-based organizations, often rely on grants from governments, foundations, and international institutions. Grant proposals are the vehicle through which they present their projects and vision to potential donors. Successful grant writing allows these organizations to access funding, which is vital for implementing projects such as clean water programs, healthcare clinics, and educational programs.

International development addresses some of the world's most pressing challenges, including poverty, hunger, disease, and environmental degradation. Grant writing enables organizations to articulate their strategies for mitigating these issues. By securing funding, they can execute initiatives that contribute to solving global problems. For example, grants have played a significant role in the fight against diseases like HIV/AIDS and malaria, as well as in disaster relief efforts in regions affected by natural disasters.

Grant-funded projects often focus on sustainability, promoting long-term positive change within communities. For instance, grants might support projects that provide vocational training to help individuals build livelihoods, or they might fund initiatives aimed at enhancing agricultural practices to ensure food security. By creating sustainable change, grant writing helps international development initiatives achieve lasting impact and reduce dependency on external aid.

The grant writing process encourages innovation and creativity in addressing complex development issues. To secure funding, organizations need to develop novel approaches and solutions that are cost-effective and efficient. This fosters a culture of innovation, leading to new technologies and practices that can be applied in international development efforts, such as renewable energy solutions or innovative educational models.

While grant writing is instrumental in international development, it comes with its own set of challenges. The demand for international development grants is high, and many organizations compete for limited funding. This results in intense competition, requiring grant writers to craft compelling proposals to stand out. International development projects are often multifaceted and require comprehensive, well-researched proposals. Grant writers must navigate complex issues and understand local contexts to create effective project plans. Also, grant writers must possess a deep understanding of the subject matter to write convincing proposals. This often necessitates collaboration with experts in various fields, adding complexity to the grant writing process.

Many grants come with specific requirements and guidelines that organizations must adhere to. Grant writers must ensure their proposals meet all compliance standards, which can be time-consuming and challenging. Understanding local cultures and contexts is crucial for international development projects. Grant writers must demonstrate cultural sensitivity in their proposals to ensure their projects are well-received and effective. To crown it all, after receiving a grant, organizations are often required to provide regular progress reports and monitor the impact of their projects. This adds an ongoing administrative burden to grant recipients.

How Lucrative is Grant Writing?

The pay for grant writers can vary significantly depending on various factors, including location, experience, the type of organization they work for, and the specific grant writing projects they handle. Here are some key considerations that affect how much grant writers are paid:

Location: The geographic location plays a crucial role in determining grant writers' salaries. Major cities and regions with a high cost of living generally offer higher salaries than areas with a lower cost of living. For example, grant writers in New York City or San Francisco may earn more than those in smaller towns or rural areas.

Experience: Grant writers with more experience tend to command higher salaries. Experienced grant writers often have a proven track record of successfully securing grants and are familiar with the intricacies of the grant application process. Entry-level grant writers may receive lower compensation initially.

Type of Organization: The type of organization that employs the grant writer can also impact their salary. Grant writers working for large, well-funded organizations or government agencies may receive higher salaries compared to those working for smaller nonprofits or start-up organizations with limited budgets.

Nonprofit vs. For-profit: Grant writers are employed by both nonprofit and for-profit organizations. While many nonprofit grant writers are paid a salary, some work on a freelance or contract basis and receive compensation on a per-grant basis. For-profit companies may also employ grant writers for different purposes, such as securing government contracts or business grants.

Education and Credentials: Grant writers with advanced degrees or relevant certifications, such as Certified Fund Raising Executive (CFRE) or Grant Professional Certified (GPC), may receive higher compensation. These credentials can demonstrate their expertise and commitment to the field.

Grant Complexity: The complexity of the grants being pursued can affect compensation. Writing grants for large, multi-year projects with complex requirements and extensive reporting may result in higher pay than writing grants for smaller, less complex projects.

Performance-Based Incentives: Some organizations offer performance-based incentives or bonuses to grant writers. These incentives can be tied to the number of grants secured or the amount of funding obtained.

Freelance vs. In-House: Freelance grant writers often set their own rates and fees, which can vary widely based on their experience and reputation. In-house grant writers typically receive a fixed salary with benefits, and their compensation structure is usually more predictable.

Industry or Sector: Grant writers working in specific industries or sectors, such as healthcare, education, or environmental conservation, may command higher salaries due to the specialized knowledge and skills required in those areas.

Market Demand: The demand for grant writers in a particular region or sector can impact salaries. High-demand areas may offer more competitive compensation packages to attract and retain experienced grant writers.

According to data available before the release of this book, the median annual salary for grant writers in the United States ranged from approximately $45,000 to $150,000, with variations depending on the factors mentioned above. However, it's important to note that salaries can change over time due to economic conditions, changes in demand for grant writers, and other factors.

Grants from a Professional Point of View

What is Grant Writing

The American Association of Grant Professionals (AAGP) has defined Grant Writing as the process of creating a compelling, well-organized, and thorough written proposal that outlines a project or program's objectives, methods, and budget, with the aim of securing financial support from grantmakers. This is an interesting definition, and it outlines the general process of grant writing. However, there are other definitions that also give better insight to what a Grant really is. The Foundation Center defines Grant Writing as the art of seeking funding through a written request. This request, usually called a grant proposal, outlines the project or program that needs funding and provides detailed information about why and how the funds will be used. This is clear, concise, and provides an explanation that anyone can understand. However this definition also falls short of substance. What we want is a definition that is all encompassing, one that tells us what it is as well as who or what is involved in the process. So, with this in mind, here is our well-rounded definition of Grant Writing:

"Grant writing is the process of preparing and submitting a written proposal, often called a grant proposal or grant application, to a funding organization, government agency, foundation, or other entity with the goal of securing financial support or resources for a specific project, program, research, or initiative. Grant writing is a critical skill for nonprofit organizations, researchers, educational institutions, and individuals seeking external funding for various purposes."

What are the types of grants available?

Grants can vary significantly in terms of the funders, their purpose, eligibility criteria, and the level of competition they pose for grant writers. This is what makes Grant Writing one of the most tasking forms of writing. Here are some common types of grants, and what sets them apart:

Foundation Grants

This type of Grant is typically provided by private philanthropic organizations, such as family foundations, community foundations, and corporate foundations. They fund a wide range of nonprofit projects and initiatives, including those related to education, healthcare, arts and culture, and social services.

Foundation grants vary in size and scope, with some offering significant funding opportunities. They often require alignment with the foundation's mission and priorities. They can be competitive, as many nonprofits seek funding from limited resources. Grant writers must thoroughly research and tailor their proposals to match the specific interests of each foundation.

Government Grants

These are provided by federal, state, or local government agencies to support a wide array of public projects, programs, and services. They can include research grants, community development grants, and more. These grants tend to have rigorous application processes and extensive reporting requirements due to the use of public funds. They may also be subject to political considerations and changing priorities. The complexity of government grant applications and the level of competition can make them challenging for grant writers. Meeting strict compliance and documentation standards is crucial to securing funding.

Corporate Grants

They are offered by businesses to support various causes, such as education, environmental sustainability, community development, and employee engagement. Corporate grants often focus on projects that align with a company's corporate social responsibility (CSR) goals. They may also involve partnerships with nonprofits or community organizations. Building strong relationships with corporations and demonstrating how a project aligns with their common objectives can be challenging. Grant writers need to elaborately showcase the mutual benefits of the partnership.

Research Grants

These types of grants are typically awarded to academic researchers and institutions to fund scientific research, experiments, studies, and investigations across various disciplines. Research grants emphasize the advancement of knowledge and innovation. They require rigorous methodologies, detailed proposals, and often involve peer review. The competition for research grants can be intense, as researchers must demonstrate the significance and potential impact of their research, as well as their ability to execute it effectively.

Programmatic Grants

As the name implies, programmatic grants are awarded to support specific programs or projects run by nonprofit organizations, government agencies, or educational institutions. These grants may focus on areas like education, healthcare, or community development. They are versatile and can vary widely in scope and scale. They are often used to address pressing social issues and community needs. In order to win grants, writers must demonstrate the feasibility and effectiveness of their proposed programs, as well as the organization's capacity to deliver on their promises.

Individual Grants or Fellowship

These are awarded directly to individuals, such as artists, writers, researchers, or students, to support their personal projects, research, or professional development. They enable individuals to pursue their creative or academic endeavors, often without the need for institutional affiliation. The competition for individual grants can be fierce, and applicants must demonstrate exceptional talent, creativity, or research potential.

A common question people ask is "which type of grant is most challenging to write proposals for?" The answer is not so simple. The most challenging type of grant for a grant writer can vary depending on their expertise and the specific project or organization they are working with. However, government grants and research grants tend to be particularly demanding due to their rigorous application processes, stringent reporting requirements, and the level of competition they often entail. Additionally, government grants may involve navigating complex bureaucracy and compliance regulations, making them especially challenging for grant writers who are less experienced in dealing with government agencies. Research grants, on the other hand, require a high level of academic rigor and the ability to convey the significance and feasibility of research projects to peer reviewers.

Grant Writing is a very competitive field and while some grant writers have had successes in securing grants, others may not have similar luck. Some even begin to wonder about the fairness of the selection process. The fact is this; the success of a proposal isn't about how much information you have in your proposal or how thorough your research was.

The fairness of the grant-giving process can vary widely depending on the specific grant program, the funding entity, and the broader context.

While many grant programs aim to be fair and impartial, there are several factors and considerations to be aware of in the way grants are given, and these factors can influence who is prioritized. It's important to note that grant-making organizations often have their own goals, priorities, and constraints, which can impact their decision-making process. It all boils down to the question; "ARE YOU FUNDABLE?"

Here are some realistic considerations that may determine if a funder will consider your proposal over others, or if you are just not the right candidate in spite of your well-written proposal:

Alignment with Grantor's Mission and Priorities: Grantors typically prioritize projects and proposals that align closely with their own mission and funding priorities. Organizations or individuals whose work closely matches these priorities are more likely to receive funding.

Competition and Limited Resources: Grant programs are often highly competitive, with many applicants vying for a limited pool of funds. Consequently, even deserving proposals may be declined due to resource constraints.

Demonstrated Need and Impact: Grantors are often interested in projects that address pressing community needs or have the potential for significant positive impact. Proposals that can demonstrate the depth of need and the potential for change may receive priority.

Capacity and Track Record: A funder may prioritize organizations or individuals with a track record of successfully implementing similar projects. This reflects the funder's confidence in the applicant's ability to deliver results.

Geographic Considerations: Some grant programs may prioritize projects in specific geographic regions, such as areas with higher poverty rates or underserved communities.

Diversity and Equity: Increasingly, grantors are emphasizing diversity, equity, and inclusion in their grant-making processes. They may prioritize projects and applicants that promote diversity and address systemic inequalities.

Transparency and Accountability: Funders prioritize applicants who can demonstrate transparency in their financial and organizational practices and who have mechanisms in place for accountability and reporting. Your reporting process MUST be comprehensive and consistent.

Innovation and Creativity: Some grant programs value innovative and creative approaches to addressing challenges. Projects that offer novel solutions or approaches may receive special consideration.

Collaboration and Partnerships: Grantors may prioritize projects that involve collaboration and partnerships with other organizations or stakeholders, as this can enhance the potential for success and impact.

Compliance and Regulations: Grantors are expected to adhere to legal and regulatory requirements. Applicants that demonstrate a clear understanding of these requirements and can navigate them effectively may have an advantage.

Grantor's Preferences and Bias: Grant decisions can sometimes be influenced by personal biases or preferences of the grant reviewers or decision-makers, despite efforts to maintain objectivity. For instance, a funder may decide to fund a faith-based organization that provides education for communities rather than a regular organization who does the same, because of a religious bias.

Timing and External Factors: External factors, such as changes in government funding priorities or economic conditions, can impact the availability and prioritization of grants.

A grant is non-refundable, and that is why so much care is taken in the selection process. Grants are different from loans, but in what way?

Grant Vs Loans and Other Funding sources

Grants are typically non-repayable funds provided by government agencies, foundations, corporations, or nonprofits to support specific projects, programs, research, or initiatives. They are intended to achieve social, educational, scientific, or charitable objectives. They are available for a wide range of purposes, including nonprofit programs, research, arts and culture, and community development. Receiving grants can enhance an organization's reputation and credibility. However, applications often face stiff competition, and not all applicants receive funding. Grants are often earmarked for particular purposes and may not be flexible.

Loans, on the other hand, are funds provided by banks, financial institutions, or individuals that must be repaid with interest. They are typically used to finance business operations, education, real estate, or personal needs. They provide immediate access to capital for various purposes and borrowers have more control over how they use the funds. Responsible repayment of loans can positively impact credit scores. Now, of course there are disadvantages as well. Loans must be repaid with interest, which can lead to financial burden and borrowers pay interest on loans, increasing the overall cost of borrowing. Eligibility for loans often depends on creditworthiness, collateral, and income. Let's take a look at other sources of funding that are NOT grants.

Equity: Equity financing involves selling shares or ownership in a company to raise capital. It doesn't require repayment, but it dilutes ownership.

Crowdfunding: There are crowdfunding platforms where companies can ask for funding. Crowdfunding platforms enable individuals or organizations to raise funds from a large number of contributors. It's accessible but may require significant marketing efforts.

Donations: These are funds provided by individuals, businesses, or philanthropic organizations for charitable or nonprofit purposes. They are typically non-repayable.

Venture Capital: Venture capitalists invest in high-growth startups in exchange for equity. They provide expertise but often seek significant control.

Angel Investors: Similar to venture capitalists, Angel investors are individuals who invest their own money in startups in exchange for equity. They offer mentorship but can be selective.

Now, that we understand what Grant Writing is, and its types, let's look at the Grant Lifecyle.

The Grant Life Cycle

Think of a grant lifecycle as the journey that a grant goes through from the initial idea to its completion. It involves several stages, each with its own set of factors and determinants. Remember that a grant is literally a sum of money allocated to an organization for the completion of a particular project. The lifecyle of the grant begins from when the idea of executing the project is conceived, conversely, the grant lifecycle ends when the project has been completed.

Let's break down the grant lifecycle with a clear and comprehensive example:

Stage 1: Identifying Funding Opportunities

Imagine you work for a nonprofit focused on environmental conservation. You research foundations and government agencies that support conservation projects. You identify a grant opportunity from a foundation that shares your passion for preserving natural habitats.

Factors and Determinants:

- Your organization's goals and needs
- Your research on potential funders
- The alignment between your project and the funder's priorities

Stage 2: Proposal Development

You carefully craft a proposal that outlines your organization's mission, the urgent need for habitat preservation, and a detailed plan for how the grant money will be used to achieve these goals.

Factors and Determinants:

- The specific requirements of the grant application

- Your project's objectives, strategies, and budget

- The clarity and persuasiveness of your proposal

Stage 3: Submission and Review

In this stage, you submit your proposal by the grant deadline. The foundation reviews it, considering factors like your project's feasibility, alignment with its mission, and the impact it can make.

Actors and Determinants:

- Meeting the application deadline

- The quality of your proposal

- The grantor's review process and criteria

Stage 4: Grant Award

You receive good news! The foundation decides to award your organization the grant. You celebrate, but now comes the important responsibility of managing the funds effectively.

Factors and Determinants:

- The grantor's decision-making process

- The availability of funds

- The competitiveness of your proposal

Stage 5: Implementation

With the grant money in hand, your team starts implementing your conservation project. You hire experts, conduct research, and begin habitat restoration work as outlined in your proposal.

Factors and Determinants:

- Staying on track with project timelines
- Managing the budget responsibly
- Addressing unexpected challenges

Stage 6: Reporting and Accountability

You periodically provide progress reports to the foundation, detailing how their funding is making a difference. You share photos, data, and success stories to show the positive changes happening in the preserved habitats.

Factors and Determinants:

- Fulfilling reporting requirements
- Demonstrating the impact of your project
- Maintaining transparency

Stage 7: Project Completion

After several months of hard work, your project reaches its completion. The habitats are thriving, and you've made a significant positive impact on the environment.

Factors and Determinants:

- Successfully achieving project goals
- Closing out the project responsibly
- Meeting all grant requirements

Stage 8: Grant Closure

You provide a final report to the foundation, summarizing the project's outcomes and financial details. You express your gratitude and provide a plan for continued conservation efforts.

Factors and Determinants:

- Completing any final reports or evaluations
- Returning unused funds, if required
- Maintaining a positive relationship with the grantor

Stage 9: Reflection and Future Planning

Your organization reflects on the grant lifecycle, celebrating successes and learning from challenges. You start researching new funding opportunities to support your ongoing conservation efforts.

Factors and Determinants:

- Evaluating the overall grant experience
- Assessing lessons learned
- Planning for future grant opportunities

It's a dynamic process that requires careful planning, effective communication, and a commitment to achieving the goals of both your organization and the grantor. Each stage has its own set of factors and determinants that influence whether your grant proposal succeeds in securing funding and ultimately makes a positive impact on your chosen cause.

Research and Preparation

After identifying the funding needs of your organization, the obvious next step is to find potential funders. So how do you find the right funders for your organization? This is where you need to be very analytical. Some organizations prefer to cast their nets wide by applying to all funding opportunities with the hope of getting funding from one or more of them. The more proposals you submit, the better your chances after all. In practice, the first thing to do is to identify websites that offer the sort of grants that your organization needs. Once you find these websites, sign up for updates, and receive prompt information on the availability of the sort of grants that interests you. here are some of the websites that offer various types of grants:

Website Name	Type of Grants	Website Link
Foundation Center (Candid)	Foundation grants	https://candid.org/
Grants.gov	Federal government grants	https://www.grants.gov/
National Institutes of Health (NIH)	Health research grants	https://grants.nih.gov/

Website Name	Type of Grants	Website Link
National Endowment for the Arts (NEA)	Arts and culture grants	https://www.arts.gov/grants
National Science Foundation (NSF)	Scientific research grants	https://www.nsf.gov/funding/
USAID	International development	https://www.usaid.gov/
Corporation for Public Broadcasting	Public media grants	https://www.cpb.org/grants
The Bill & Melinda Gates Foundation	Global health and education	https://www.gatesfoundation.org/

Website Name	Type of Grants	Website Link
The Kellogg Foundation	Social and racial equity	https://www.wkkf.org/
The Robert Wood Johnson Foundation	Health and healthcare	https://www.rwjf.org/
The Andrew W. Mellon Foundation	Arts and humanities	https://mellon.org/
The Ford Foundation	Social justice and equality	https://www.fordfoundation.org/
National Geographic Society	Science and exploration	https://www.nationalgeographic.org/grants
National Endowment for the	Humanities grants	https://www.neh.gov/grants

Website Name	Type of Grants	Website Link
Humanities		
U.S. Department of Education	Education grants	https://www2.ed.gov/fund/grant/find/edpicks.html
National Aeronautics and Space Administration (NASA)	Space and science research	https://www.nasa.gov/content/grants-funding-opportunities
The Getty Foundation	Arts and cultural heritage	https://www.getty.edu/foundation/
Environmental Protection Agency (EPA)	Environmental grants	https://www.epa.gov/grants
The MacArthur	Global challenges	https://www.macfound.org/

Website Name	Type of Grants	Website Link
Foundation		
National Oceanic and Atmospheric Administration (NOAA)	Ocean and atmospheric research	https://www.grants.gov/web/grants/view-opportunity.html?oppId=332161
U.S. Department of Justice	Criminal justice grants	https://www.justice.gov/grants
National Institutes of Standards and Technology (NIST)	Science and technology	https://www.nist.gov/oam/what-we-do/technology-partnerships
National Endowment	Financial education	https://www.nefe.org/

Website Name	Type of Grants	Website Link
for Financial Education (NEFE)		
Environmental Research & Education Foundation (EREF)	Environmental research	https://erefdn.org/research-grants/
National Park Service	Conservation and history	https://www.nps.gov/subjects/youth programs/apply-for-a-grant.htm
U.S. Department of Housing and Urban Development (HUD)	Housing and community development	https://www.hud.gov/program_offic es/comm_planning/grants
National	Cancer research	https://www.cancer.gov/grants-

Website Name	Type of Grants	Website Link
Cancer Institute (NCI)	grants	training
The Knight Foundation	Journalism and communities	https://knightfoundation.org/
National Endowment for Democracy (NED)	Democracy and governance	https://www.ned.org/fellowships/

How to Build Relationships with Funders

Building and maintaining strong relationships with funders is crucial for the sustainability of nonprofit organizations. The first step to achieving a relationship with funders is to Identify funders whose mission and priorities align with your organization's work. It's essential to ensure a natural fit between your mission and their funding interests. The next step is to reach out to them, but when reaching out to potential funders, tailor your communications to their specific interests and goals. Show that you've done your homework and understand their priorities. Try to be transparent about your organization's goals, challenges, and accomplishments. Funders appreciate honesty and open communication. Always keep your funders informed about your organization's progress and impact. Provide regular updates on how their support is making a difference.

On occasions, invite funders to visit your organization's facilities and programs. Face-to-face meetings can help build a deeper connection and understanding. Listen to your funders. Understand their expectations and concerns. Ask for their feedback on your organization's work. When necessary, express gratitude and appreciation for the support you receive. Acknowledge funders in your publications, events, and annual reports.

Highlight success stories and testimonials from individuals who have benefited from your programs. These real-life examples can be powerful in conveying impact. Do not wait for them to ask for information on projects, rather, provide evidence of how their funding has led to positive outcomes. Use data and metrics to show the tangible effects of their support and meet all reporting requirements promptly and comprehensively. Funders rely on these reports to evaluate the impact of their investment.

To show how much you value them, invite funders to participate in advisory roles, committees, or discussions related to your organization's strategy or projects. Their input can be valuable. Some funders may prefer in-person meetings, while others may prefer digital communication. Be flexible and adapt to their preferred communication methods.

Building strong relationships with funders takes time. Focus on the long-term benefits of these partnerships rather than immediate gains. It becomes worthwhile as time progresses. Be accountable for how you use their funds. Demonstrate that you are responsible stewards of their investment. Remember that funders are more likely to continue supporting organizations with which they have strong, mutually beneficial relationships.

Components of Grant Writing: The Boiler plate method

Grant writing can be very repetitive, especially if you do it as a full time job for the same organization. It becomes really boring and difficult to really outdo yourself. This is human nature and isn't your fault obviously. That's why it is important to devise means to enable you write grant proposals faster and better. The most efficient way is by creating a boilerplate.

The question is, What is a boilerplate?

The boilerplate method in grant writing involves using standardized components or content in grant proposals. These components are pre-written, reusable sections of text that provide general information about an organization, its mission, and other common elements. The boilerplate method can be an efficient way to save time and ensure consistency in grant writing, but it also has its pros and cons.

Typically, a grant proposal should have the following components:

- Executive Summary
- Statement of Need

- Goals and Objectives

- Program Description

- Budget and Financial Information

- Evaluation Plan

- Sustainability Plan

- Appendices and Supporting Documents

A boilerplate has all these information pre-written as a template and stored in a computer or hard drive. Whenever the grant writer wants to apply for a grant, they simple open the boilerplate and simply edit and customize it to suit the requirements of the funder. Here are some factors to consider when using a boilerplate:

Relevance: Ensure that the boilerplate content is relevant to the specific grant proposal. It may require customization to align with the funder's priorities.

Consistency: Use boilerplate content to maintain a consistent voice and message throughout various grant proposals.

Customization: Customize boilerplate sections to address the unique needs and goals of each grant application.

Alignment with Funder's Priorities: Tailor the boilerplate to match the specific priorities and requirements of each funder.

Accuracy: Keep boilerplate content up to date to reflect the organization's current status and achievements.

Boilerplates have been used by many organizations for years and they are very effective. They certainly have their ups and downs so it is important to pay attention to details when creating or using a boilerplate for your organization because it may affect your overall success. If you make mistakes in your boilerplate, you would have to reuse a template that has multiple mistakes on them over and over again. This will certainly make you lose a ton of opportunities. Here are the pros and cons of using a Boilerplate:

Pros of the Boilerplate Method:

Time Efficiency: Boilerplate content can significantly reduce the time required to write a grant proposal, especially for sections that don't change often.

Consistency: Using standardized content ensures that the organization's key messages and information remain consistent across multiple proposals.

Resource Efficiency: It minimizes the need to recreate content for common sections, allowing grant writers to focus more on tailoring the proposal to meet the specific needs of the funder.

Accurate Information: Boilerplate sections can be regularly updated to ensure accuracy, reducing the risk of including outdated information.

Cons of the Boilerplate Method:

Lack of Customization: Over-reliance on boilerplate content may lead to proposals that lack the necessary customization to effectively address the funder's unique requirements.

Potential for Inconsistency: If boilerplate content is not consistently updated or if it becomes outdated, it can lead to inconsistencies and inaccuracies in grant proposals.

Limited Adaptability: Some funders may have strict formatting or content requirements that are not easily accommodated by boilerplate sections.

Risk of Stale Content: Boilerplate text can become overused and may appear stale or uninspiring to reviewers.

Balancing boilerplate content with fresh, tailored information is essential to create compelling and effective grant proposals.

Now Let's take a dive into the components of Grant Proposals

But before we do, let's introduce three fictional organizations that we will be using as our samples.

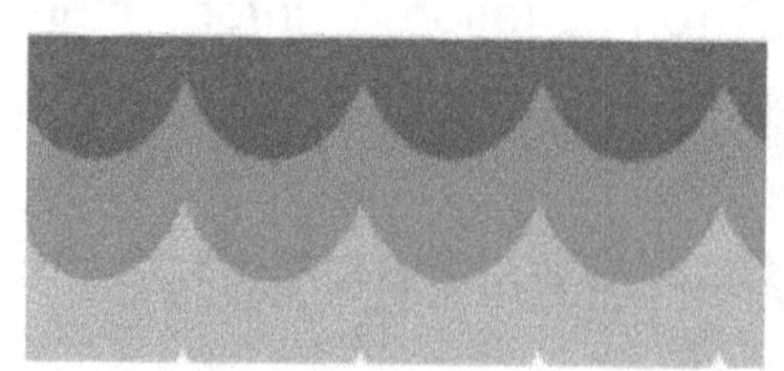

Executive Summary

An executive summary in grant writing is a succinct, well-structured document that encapsulates the core elements of a grant proposal. It offers a comprehensive yet concise overview of the project or program for which funding is sought, including its objectives, significance, approach, and budgetary considerations. It is the first thing a funder looks at in order to get a first understanding of what your proposal is all about.

The Purpose of an executive summary in grant writing is to:

Engage grant reviewers and funders by presenting a compelling introduction to the proposal, encouraging them to delve into the details.

Offer a concise summary of the proposed project's key components, such as its goals, target population, methods, and expected outcomes.

- Emphasize the significance and impact of the project, underlining why it aligns with the funder's priorities and deserves their support.
- Provide a summary of the project's budget, including the total funding request and a high-level breakdown of major budget categories.

- Tailor the proposed program to align with the specific interests, goals, and guidelines of the grant-making organization or foundation.
- Enable grant reviewers to quickly assess the proposal's suitability and alignment with their mission, saving them time in the initial review process.
- Demonstrate the grant writer's ability to communicate complex ideas clearly and persuasively, instilling confidence in the proposal's quality.

The ideal length of an executive summary can vary depending on the specific guidelines provided by the grant-making organization. However, a typical executive summary in grant writing is often recommended to be concise, spanning approximately one to two pages. It should be long enough to convey the necessary information but short enough to maintain the reader's engagement and clarity.

First-time grant writers often make very critical mistakes when creating their executive summary and even a small mistake can cause the organization to lose the funder's attention.

Most Frequent Mistakes Made When Writing an Executive Summary

- Using jargon or technical language in the executive summary can make it challenging for readers who are not experts in the field to understand the proposal's core concepts. In other words, write for humans! There's a good chance that your funder is not a scholar, a scientist, or a robot.

- Failing to present information in a clear and straightforward manner can result in confusion. Grant writers should strive for clarity in language and structure.

- Some executive summaries may lack critical elements such as a clear problem statement, expected outcomes, or a budget summary. All essential components should be included.

- Using a generic executive summary for multiple grant applications without tailoring it to each funder's priorities and guidelines can lead to missed opportunities. People who completely rely on boiler plates often make this mistake.

- Including excessive detail in the executive summary defeats its purpose. It should provide an overview rather than delving into minute specifics.

- An executive summary should capture the reader's attention and interest. Being too dry or uninteresting can discourage reviewers from continuing to the full proposal. So, for the love of God add some life to it!

- It should go without saying that the executive summary should align with the content and priorities presented in the full proposal. Inconsistencies between the two can raise concerns about the proposal's integrity.
- An effective executive summary should end with a compelling call to action, emphasizing the urgency and importance of the project. Neglecting this can reduce its impact.
- Typos, grammatical errors, and inconsistencies can detract from the professionalism and credibility of the proposal. It's essential to thoroughly proofread the executive summary.
- The executive summary is not merely a summary of the proposal; it's a tool for making a persuasive case for funding. Grant writers often underestimate its importance in the decision-making process.
- An outdated executive summary can result in inaccuracies and missed opportunities. Grant writers should update it to reflect the organization's current status and achievements.
- While brevity is essential, the executive summary should provide enough information to convey the project's significance and potential impact. Being too vague can leave readers with unanswered questions.

Here are some examples of an executive summary for our earlier mentioned non-profits.

The Girl Child Education Initiative

The "Girl Child Education" initiative is dedicated to driving change where it matters most, nurturing the minds and futures of our young girls, and creating a brighter, more equitable world for us all. millions of girl children are still denied the transformative power of quality education. We represent a relentless force for change. (You may provide statistics as well as your organization's unique position)

Our mission is clear: to break down the barriers that limit the potential of girl children through quality education. We envision a world where every girl child, regardless of her circumstances, has access to education, the power to make choices, and the ability to shape her own destiny.

Too many girl children face obstacles that hinder their educational journey, such as cultural biases, economic disparities, and unequal access to quality schools. We acknowledge these challenges, and we are determined to overcome them. (Include what makes your program extraordinary)

We understand that transformation begins with quality education. We partner with schools and communities, providing essential resources and support to ensure girls can access education without fear or discrimination. Our tailored programs focus on:

- **Scholarships:** Enabling girls to access quality education from primary to tertiary levels.
- **Mentorship:** Cultivating leadership skills and empowering girls to dream beyond the constraints of tradition.
- **Community Engagement:** Building awareness and advocating for equal educational opportunities.

Our impact is both immediate and enduring. Over the last five years:

- 99% of our scholarship recipients have completed primary and secondary education.
- 82% have forged their paths to higher education or vocational training.

– Our mentorship programs have incubated the leaders of tomorrow, as our alumni are now leading transformative initiatives in their communities.

We seek a total funding of $500,000 to continue and expand our initiatives. This will support scholarship programs, mentorship activities, community outreach, and the establishment of new educational centers.

We urge you to join us in this transformative journey. By supporting "Girl Child Education," you contribute to a world where every girl child's potential is realized. Together, we can break barriers and empower future generations.

Feed the Children Initiative

Feed The Children Initiative is steadfast in its mission - to end childhood hunger, one meal at a time. Our vision is even bolder - a world where every child not only survives but thrives, free from the shackles of hunger. (provide organizational information)

According to recent data:

- 1 in 9 children worldwide, approximately 821 million, go to bed hungry.
- In the regions we serve, nearly 70% of families struggle with food insecurity.
- Childhood malnutrition remains a critical issue, impacting growth and cognitive development.

Feed The Children Initiative stands out in the fight against childhood hunger due to its:

Global Reach: We operate in 10 countries, delivering meals and supplies to thousands of children and families each day.

Lasting Impact: Our comprehensive approach empowers communities to escape hunger's grasp and build a sustainable future.

Education Focus: We believe in the power of education to break the cycle of poverty and hunger. We support children's access to quality education, opening doors to a brighter future.

Over the last year, we've provided over 3 million meals to hungry children and families. Our programs have empowered more than 5,000 families to become self-sufficient and escape the cycle of hunger. We've enabled 2,500 children to access quality education, offering them a pathway out of poverty. We don't just provide meals, we also empower communities and support education, breaking the cycle of hunger. Our organization operates across 10 countries, making an impact on a global scale. Our programs focus on long-term solutions, ensuring that communities can thrive independently.

To continue our mission and amplify our impact, we seek a grant of $2,000,000. This investment will enable us to reach more children, deliver more meals, and create lasting change.

Feed The Children Initiative is not just a nonprofit; it's a lifeline, a promise to millions of children. By partnering with us, you become a driving force behind the solution to childhood hunger.

Together, we can create a world where no child goes to bed hungry, where dreams are nurtured, and where potential knows no bounds.

Statement of Need

The statement of need provides a comprehensive explanation of the problem or need that the proposed project or program aims to address. It outlines the current challenges, issues, or gaps within a community or organization, presenting a clear and compelling case for why the project is necessary. Here are some essential reasons why we write a statement of need:

- It justifies the project's existence by demonstrating a pressing and unmet need. This section persuades the grant-making organization that the proposed project is the right solution to a significant problem.

- It informs funders about the specific issues or challenges the project seeks to tackle. It educates them on the context and magnitude of the problem, ensuring they understand why their support is crucial.

- By providing detailed information about the need, it can evoke empathy and a sense of urgency in the grant reviewers or funders, encouraging them to take action.

- It ensures that the project aligns with the priorities and focus areas of the grant-making organization. This helps in demonstrating that the project and the funder's mission are in harmony.

- It showcases that the organization has conducted thorough research to understand the problem, often incorporating data, statistics, and expert opinions to support the claims made in the statement of need.

- It also provides an opportunity to emphasize the organization's expertise and understanding of the issue, bolstering its credibility as a capable and knowledgeable entity to address the problem.

Key Elements of a Statement of Need

To write an effective statement of need there are standards that must be followed:

- First, begin with a concise, clear, and compelling statement of the problem or need that the project aims to address. Define the issue in straightforward terms.

- Provide context and background information to help funders understand the problem's history, scope, and significance. Explain why the issue is relevant and timely.

- Include relevant statistics, research findings, and data to substantiate the existence and extent of the problem. Use credible sources and cite your references.

- Describe how the problem affects the specific population or community that the project will serve. Highlight the consequences and challenges faced by this group.

- Explain the involvement of key stakeholders or community members in identifying the problem and in shaping the project's goals and strategies.

- Discuss the existing gaps and limitations in the current services or solutions available to address the problem. Explain why current efforts fall short.

- Emphasize how the project aligns with your organization's mission and goals and how addressing this need is in line with your core values.

- Convey the urgency of the situation and the need for immediate action. Explain why addressing this issue cannot wait.

- Provide demographic information about the target population, such as age, gender, income level, and geographic location, to give funders a comprehensive understanding.

- Clearly articulate the negative consequences and potential risks if the problem is not addressed. Paint a picture of what the future might look like without intervention.

Tips for Writing a Professional Statement of Need

Be Concise: Keep your statement of need focused and concise. Avoid unnecessary jargon or lengthy explanations.

Use Persuasive Language: Craft your language to persuade funders of the urgency and significance of the problem. Be passionate and compelling in your description.

Use Visuals: Incorporate charts, graphs, and visuals to present data in a clear and engaging manner. Visuals can make statistics more accessible.

Cite Sources: Ensure that all data and statistics are properly cited, providing credibility to your claims.

Tell a Story: Weave a narrative that illustrates the problem by sharing stories or case studies of individuals or communities impacted by the issue.

Avoid Assumptions: Base your statements on verified data and avoid making unsupported assumptions.

Tailor to the Funder: Customize the statement of need to align with the specific priorities and interests of the grant-making organization.

Review and Revise: Carefully proofread and edit the statement of need to eliminate errors and ensure clarity. Seek feedback from colleagues or peers.

Connect to the Solution: Close the statement of need by connecting the problem to the proposed project, making a clear case for how the project addresses the identified need.

Stay Focused: Stay on-topic and avoid deviating into unrelated issues or providing excessive background information. Stick to the core problem and its significance.

Here is a statement of need for the fictional non-profit Save The Ocean.

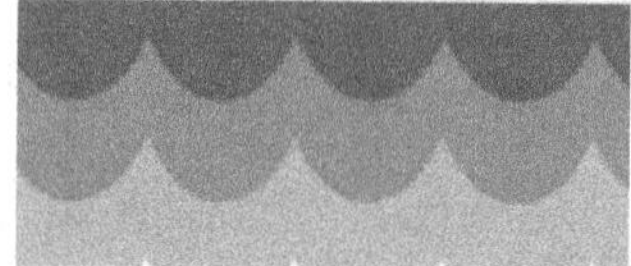

Concise Problem Statement: The world's oceans, which sustain all life on Earth, face a dire and escalating crisis. Our "Save the Ocean" initiative confronts the critical problem of ocean degradation and its devastating impacts on the environment, communities, and biodiversity. We urgently seek support to reverse this trend and secure the future of our oceans.

Context and Background: Our planet's oceans, covering over 70% of its surface, play a pivotal role in regulating climate, supporting diverse ecosystems, and providing sustenance to billions of people. However, this vital ecosystem is in peril. Rampant pollution, overfishing, habitat destruction, and climate change have pushed our oceans to the brink of collapse. The consequences are far-reaching, affecting marine life, coastal communities, and the world at large.

Relevant Statistics and Data: The evidence is stark:

- Over 8 million tons of plastic enter the oceans each year, threatening marine life and ecosystems (UNEP).
- A third of global fish stocks are overfished, jeopardizing a critical food source for billions (FAO).
- Ocean acidification, driven by carbon emissions, threatens coral reefs and marine food chains (NOAA).
- Rising sea levels due to melting polar ice caps imperil coastal communities and economies (IPCC).

Affect on Communities: Coastal communities and vulnerable populations face the brunt of these challenges. Declining fish stocks mean lost livelihoods, while plastic pollution and rising seas threaten homes and health. Traditional ways of life are in jeopardy, leaving these communities at a crossroads.

Involvement of Stakeholders: Our initiative is rooted in collaboration with key stakeholders, including marine scientists, local communities, environmental organizations, and policymakers. Their insights and involvement have informed the development of our comprehensive ocean conservation program.

Existing Gaps and Limitations: Current conservation efforts, while admirable, fall short of addressing the full scope of ocean degradation. Gaps exist in waste management infrastructure, sustainable fishing practices, and the comprehensive protection of marine ecosystems. Urgent intervention is essential to bridge these gaps.

Alignment with Mission and Goals: Our "Save the Ocean" initiative aligns seamlessly with our organization's mission to safeguard the environment and protect vulnerable communities. It resonates with our core values of environmental stewardship and social responsibility. By addressing the ocean crisis, we fulfill our commitment to a sustainable, equitable future.

Urgency of the Situation: The urgency of this situation cannot be overstated. Every day without intervention brings us closer to a point of no return. Irreversible damage to marine ecosystems, communities, and the global climate is on the horizon. Immediate action is imperative to safeguard the oceans and secure our planet's future.

Demographic Information: Our project targets coastal communities, particularly those in developing nations, where livelihoods and food security depend on the ocean. These communities are often characterized by low income, reliance on subsistence fishing, and inadequate infrastructure to combat the impacts of ocean degradation.

Consequences of Inaction: Without swift action, the consequences are dire. We face a future marked by collapsed fish stocks, coastal inundation, and loss of biodiversity. Vulnerable communities will experience heightened poverty and food insecurity, while global climate regulation is compromised.

The "Save the Ocean" initiative seeks to rescue our oceans from the brink of catastrophe, protect vulnerable communities, and preserve the delicate balance of life on Earth. With your support, we can embark on a mission to ensure the oceans thrive and endure for generations to come.

Goals and Objectives

Goals are the overarching, broad, and long-term outcomes that an organization or project aims to achieve. They provide a high-level direction for the project and help define its purpose and ultimate impact. Goals are often aligned with an organization's mission and represent the big picture vision for what the project intends to accomplish.

Objectives are specific, measurable, achievable, relevant, and time-bound (SMART) targets that support the realization of the overarching goals. They break down the goals into concrete, actionable steps. Objectives provide a roadmap for how the organization or project will reach its goals and serve as the foundation for monitoring progress and evaluating success.

Goals and objectives provide clarity by defining what the project seeks to achieve and the specific steps to get there. They help stakeholders and funders understand the project's direction.

Here are some valuable tips on how to write Goals and objectives that will make your proposal stand out.

- Goals should be broad and reflect the long-term outcomes or impact you aim to achieve. Avoid getting into specifics at this stage. While goals are broad, they should still be specific enough to convey a clear sense of what you want to achieve. Use concise language.

- Ensure that your goals align with your organization's mission and the specific grant program's priorities or focus areas.
- Start your goals with action verbs like "to reduce," "to increase," or "to enhance." This makes your goals more action-oriented.
- While goals should be ambitious, they should also be realistic and achievable within the project's scope and timeframe.
- Objectives should be Specific, Measurable, Achievable, Relevant, and Time-bound (SMART). This ensures clarity and accountability. Each objective should focus on a single, specific outcome. Avoid combining multiple outcomes in a single objective.
- Use numerical values or percentages to make your objectives measurable. For example, "Increase literacy rates by 15% among third-grade students."
- Clearly connect each objective to the corresponding goal. Show how achieving the objective contributes to the overall goal.
- Describe how you will measure the achievement of the objective. What data or metrics will be used to assess success?
- Write objectives in plain language to ensure that all stakeholders, including reviewers, can easily understand what is expected.
- If you have multiple objectives, prioritize them based on their importance and relevance to the overall goal. Not all objectives are equally critical.

– If your project has multiple phases or steps, consider the logical sequence of objectives. Each objective should build upon the previous one.

Here's an example of Goals and Objectives for our fictional Non-profit, Save the Ocean.

Goal 1: Marine Ecosystem Conservation

Objective 1: By the end of Year 2, our efforts will increase coral reef health in the targeted region by 15% through coral restoration programs, as measured by coral coverage and biodiversity indices.

Objective 2: Within three years, we would have reduced ocean plastic pollution in the project area by 20% based on the amount of marine litter collected annually during beach clean-up events.

Goal 2: Sustainable Fishing Practices

Objective 1: Within the first year, we will provide training and resources to 50% of local fishermen in the community to promote sustainable fishing practices, as measured by a 10% reduction in overfishing within the targeted fishing zone.

Objective 2: Over a four-year period, we will achieve a 25% increase in income for participating fishermen by improving fishing efficiency and access to fair markets, as measured by annual income data.

Goal 3: Ocean Literacy and Advocacy

Objective 1: Within the next two years, we will develop and deliver an ocean education program to reach 80% of local schools and engage 70% of the community's youth, as measured by student participation and knowledge assessments.

Objective 2: Within three years, mobilize a community of 1,000 advocates for marine conservation through educational workshops and outreach, as measured by the number of participants engaged in advocacy initiatives.

Goal 4: Coastal Community Resilience

Objective 1: By Year 2, we will have enhanced the resilience of 60% of vulnerable coastal households by implementing climate adaptation strategies, as measured by the number of households with improved infrastructure and livelihood diversification.

Objective 2: Within four years, our program will reduce the risk of coastal erosion for 80% of targeted coastal communities by implementing nature-based solutions, as measured by the extent of stabilized coastlines.

Monitoring and Evaluation

Each objective will be assessed through a combination of quantitative and qualitative data. We will utilize data on coral coverage, biodiversity, marine litter collected, fishing records, income data, student assessments, participant numbers, and infrastructure improvements. Regular evaluations will be conducted to measure our progress, identify challenges, and adapt strategies accordingly. The effectiveness of our objectives will be assessed annually, with adjustments made to ensure the achievement of our overarching goals. Our organization is committed to transparent reporting and accountability.

Priority: Objectives will be prioritized based on their relevance and significance to the overall goals. The preservation of marine ecosystems and the reduction of plastic pollution are of utmost importance, followed by sustainable fishing practices, ocean literacy, and community resilience, in that order.

Program Description

It outlines the program's structure, components, objectives, activities, target population, and anticipated outcomes. The program description serves as a critical component of the grant proposal, offering a comprehensive portrayal of the project to grant-makers and stakeholders. It is basically like a detailed story that explains why your project is a great idea and how it's going to make things better.

The key element of a Program Description includes these:

1. The name of your program
2. Program overview
3. Your goals and objectives
4. Target population
5. Activities and intervention
6. Timeline
7. Partnerships and collaborations
8. Overview of budget
9. Evaluation and Measurement of success
10. Sustainability
11. Community impact

12. Challenges and risks

13. Organizational Capacity

14. Alignment with Funder's Priorities

Essential Tips on How to write a Program Description

- Use clear and straightforward language. Avoid jargon or complex terms that may confuse readers. Keep your sentences and paragraphs concise.

- Engage the reader by framing your program as a compelling story. Explain the problem or need, the solution your program provides, and the positive impact it will have.

- Organize your program description with headings and subheadings to make it easy for readers to find information and navigate the text.

- Emphasize how the program will benefit the target population or community. Explain why it's important and how it will improve their lives.

- Provide concrete examples of program activities and their expected outcomes. Use real stories, if possible, to illustrate your points.

- Clearly connect the program's objectives with the activities you plan to undertake. Show how each activity supports the achievement of specific objectives.

- Acknowledge potential challenges or obstacles your program may face and describe how you will overcome them. This demonstrates preparedness.

- Explain what sets your program apart from others addressing similar issues. Highlight any innovative approaches or distinctive features.

- Back up your claims with data, research findings, and evidence that support the need for your program and its effectiveness.

- Present your program in a realistic and achievable manner. Avoid making exaggerated claims or promises that cannot be fulfilled.

- If you are collaborating with other organizations or partners, mention them and describe how these collaborations will enhance the program's impact.

- Ensure that your program description aligns with the goals and priorities of the grant-making organization. Tailor your description to their specific requirements.

- Clarify how you will measure the success of your program. Describe the evaluation methods and metrics that will be used.

- Put yourself in the shoes of the grant reviewer. What information would they need to understand and support your program? Provide it clearly.
- While acknowledging challenges, maintain a positive tone throughout your description. Convey enthusiasm and confidence in the program's potential impact.

Now, let's put all of these into practice. Here is an example of a Program Description:

"Girl Child Education" is a passionate and dedicated non-profit organization committed to making a transformative difference in the lives of young girls and their communities. Our mission is to break down barriers and empower girls through education, enabling them to reach their full potential and contribute to a more equitable world.

The Problem

In many parts of the world, millions of girls face formidable barriers to accessing quality education. These barriers include poverty, gender discrimination, early marriage, cultural norms, and lack of infrastructure. The result is a stark gender disparity in educational opportunities and a cycle of disadvantage for girls and their communities.

Our Solution

Empowering the Future: Our Innovative Program

At "Girl Child Education," we believe that education is a powerful tool for change. Our program focuses on addressing the specific challenges that hinder girls' access to education and seeks to create a more equitable world by:

1. Providing Scholarships and Financial Support:

We offer scholarships and financial support to girls who would otherwise be unable to afford school fees, uniforms, and books. Our goal is to make education accessible to every girl, regardless of her economic background.

2. Encouraging Community Engagement:

We work closely with communities to raise awareness about the importance of girls' education. By involving parents, community leaders, and teachers, we create a supportive environment for girls to thrive.

3. Girls' Mentorship Programs

We offer mentorship programs that inspire and guide girls toward their educational goals. These programs provide role models and support networks that motivate girls to stay in school.

Expected Outcomes

Our holistic approach to girls' education aims to bring about significant and measurable outcomes:

Increase in Girls' Enrollment: We anticipate a 30% increase in girls' enrollment in the next three years in the communities we serve.

Reduction in Dropout Rates: By providing financial support and mentorship, we aim to reduce the dropout rate among girls by 20% within the first year.

Improved Academic Performance: We expect an average increase of 15% in girls' academic performance, with more girls transitioning to higher education.

Community Advocacy: We aim to engage at least 80% of community members in advocating for girls' education, leading to a cultural shift in support of girls' schooling.

Overcoming Challenges

We understand that challenges may arise, including cultural resistance, economic constraints, and logistical difficulties. To address these, we have developed strategies for community sensitization, financial sustainability, and adaptive program management. Our experience in similar projects has equipped us to tackle obstacles head-on.

Our Uniqueness

"Girl Child Education" stands out for its innovative approach, which combines financial support, mentorship, and community engagement to address the root causes of girls' educational exclusion. Our organization's deep roots in the communities we serve and our close collaboration with local partners enable us to create sustainable change.

Data and Evidence

Our program is grounded in extensive research that demonstrates the powerful impact of girls' education on not only individual lives but also on communities and nations. We use data, such as literacy rates and girls' academic achievements, to continuously refine and improve our program.

Realism and Achievability

We have set realistic and attainable goals, supported by our proven track record in similar projects. We are confident in our ability to create a meaningful and lasting impact.

Collaborative Efforts

We collaborate with local schools, community organizations, and government bodies to maximize our program's reach and effectiveness. Our strong partnerships enable us to leverage resources and expertise for the benefit of girls.

Alignment with Funders' Goals

Our program aligns seamlessly with the goals and priorities of grant-making organizations. We are committed to tailoring our program to meet the specific requirements of funders to ensure a strong partnership.

Measurement of Success

We have a robust evaluation plan in place, including pre-and post-program assessments, community surveys, and academic performance tracking. We are dedicated to transparently reporting our results and impact to our funders.

Conclusion

"Girl Child Education" is more than an organization; it's a movement dedicated to changing the future for girls and their communities. We invite you to join us in this transformative journey, where every girl's education is a step toward a more equitable world. We are optimistic, prepared, and enthusiastic about the profound impact our program can make in the lives of girls and the communities we serve. Together, we can empower girls through education and create a brighter future for all.

Budget and Financial Information

The budget and financial information section serves several important purposes. It demonstrates that your organization is financially responsible and capable of managing the funds effectively. This is essential for gaining the trust of potential funders. It also provides a comprehensive breakdown of the costs associated with the project, allowing grant reviewers to understand how the funds will be utilized. This transparency helps assess the feasibility of the proposed activities.

The budget shows that the financial plan is aligned with the objectives and activities outlined in the proposal. It ensures that funds are allocated to support the achievement of the proposed goals. Grant reviewers use the budget to assess whether the project is financially realistic. They look for evidence that the budget aligns with the scale and complexity of the proposed project. It may also reveal the organization's ability to leverage funds from multiple sources, such as in-kind contributions, matching grants, or partnerships, which can enhance the project's impact.

The budget and financial information section ensures that the project complies with legal and ethical financial standards. This is particularly important for non-profit organizations.

Grant-making organizations often have specific budget format requirements. Providing a clear and well-organized budget ensures that your proposal meets these requirements. Budgets also help funders assess the cost-effectiveness of the project and make informed decisions about allocating resources.

Key elements of Budget and Financial Information

Money talks are always complex and require more attentiveness as well as a breakdown in terms of allocation, and usage. Here are some key elements that you would likely provide critical analysis for when creating a budget.

- **Total Project Budget:** A clear and concise summary of the total budget for the project. This includes all anticipated income and expenditures.

- **Income Sources:** Detailed information on all organizational sources of income, which may include the grant amount requested, contributions from the organization, other grants or donations, in-kind contributions, and any earned income (e.g., program fees).

- **Expenditure Categories:** A breakdown of the project's costs into specific categories. Common expenditure categories include personnel, supplies, equipment, travel, training, and overhead.

- **Personnel Costs:** A detailed list of the project's staff, their roles, and their salaries or wages. This may include both full-time and part-time employees, consultants, and contractors.

- **Fringe Benefits:** If applicable, information on fringe benefits for staff, such as health insurance, retirement contributions, and payroll taxes.

- **Supplies and Materials:** A breakdown of costs associated with supplies, materials, or equipment required for the project.

- **Travel:** Details on anticipated travel costs, including transportation, lodging, meals, and other related expenses.

- **Training and Professional Development:** Costs related to training and professional development of staff or participants, including registration fees, materials, and travel.

- **Contractual Services:** Costs associated with outsourcing certain project tasks to external service providers, such as consultants or trainers.

- **Indirect or Overhead Costs:** Allocation of indirect costs or overhead costs, such as rent, utilities, and administrative support, as a percentage of the total budget.

- **In-Kind Contributions:** Documentation of any in-kind contributions, such as donated goods, services, or volunteer time.

- **Matching Funds:** If required by the grant-maker, details about any matching funds or cost-sharing arrangements, and the sources of these funds.

- **Budget Narrative:** An accompanying narrative that explains and justifies the budget. This narrative provides context for each line item, such as explaining the need for specific expenditures and the method of calculating costs.

- **Budget Period:** Specify the budget period, which may cover the entire project duration or a specific timeframe, such as a fiscal year.

- **Currency and Units:** Clearly state the currency used and any relevant units of measurement (e.g., hours, quantities) for cost items.

- **Notes and Assumptions:** Include any additional notes or assumptions that provide context to the budget, such as inflation rates, salary increases, or other variables affecting costs.

- **Cost-Effectiveness:** Demonstrate that the project is cost-effective by showing how the proposed budget aligns with the expected outcomes and impact.

- **Budget Summary:** A summarized view of income and expenditures to provide an at-a-glance understanding of the financial plan.

- **Budget Justification:** An explanation of how the budget aligns with the project's goals, activities, and objectives, and how the project activities and outcome is worth the amount of money asked for.

Sample of Budget for our fictional non-profit, Feed the Children

Category	Item	Description	Total Budget (USD)
Program Expenses			$7,500,000
	Food Distribution	Purchase and transport of food supplies	$4,000,000
	Education and Training	Training programs for beneficiaries	$1,500,000
	Healthcare Services	Medical supplies, clinics, and health programs	$1,000,000
	Community Development	Infrastructure, clean water, sanitation projects	$1,000,000
Personnel Costs		Salaries, benefits, and payroll taxes	$1,800,000
	Program Staff	Project coordinators, field officers, trainers	$1,200,000

Category	Item	Description	Total Budget (USD)
	Administrative Staff	Administrative and support staff	$600,000
Overhead and Administration		Office rent, utilities, insurance, and office supplies	$500,000
Fundraising and Marketing			$600,000
	Fundraising Campaigns	Fundraising events, campaigns, and marketing	$500,000
	Public Relations	Promotional materials, public awareness campaigns	$100,000
Evaluation and Research		Impact assessments, surveys, and research	$150,000

Category	Item	Description	Total Budget (USD)
		projects	
Contingency		Unforeseen expenses and emergencies	$150,000
Total Project Budget			$10,700,000

In this budget, we have accounted for program expenses related to food distribution, education, healthcare, and community development. Personnel costs include salaries and benefits for program and administrative staff. Overhead covers office-related expenses, while fundraising and marketing are essential for generating future funding. Evaluation and research contribute to ongoing program improvement. A contingency fund is included to address unexpected challenges.

This detailed budget demonstrates the organization's commitment to financial transparency and sound fiscal management. While this is a standard template it can be more elaborate. When creating a budget, you can adapt the template to suit the specific programs, add other variables such as timelines, travel, per diems, hired labors, consultant fees, rented or purchased equipment, etc. Be as transparent as possible and conduct research on the actual cost of things before drafting a budget so that you do not over bloat or underestimate the actual cost. Understand that the funder is interested in funding specific programmatic activities that have measurable outcomes and adds to the project itself and is not interested in funding your lifestyle, your new office, and all those regular organizational expenses and operational costs.

This brings us to the question, what exactly do funders prefer to fund? The answer would give you better insight on what you should add to your budget and what you shouldn't when asking for grants.

What do funders Prefer to fund?

A lot of grant writers make the common mistake of adding certain things to their budget that grantors do not want to spend their hard earned money on. Funders typically have a project in mind and only want to fund activities that directly affect the project. Grants are not free money to be used for random activities. This is where accountability comes into the picture. Funders want to know that they can trust you with their money and that at the end of the project lifecycle, their needs would be achieved. Grants are not Lottery monies!

Here's a small list of the things funders expect to fund and the things that may cause them to reject your grant proposal.

Preferred to Fund	May or May Not Fund	Do Not Prefer to Fund
Program Activities	Office Rent	Lobbying Activities
Personnel Salaries	Supplies and Materials	Political Campaigns
Project-Specific Travel	Consultants and Experts	Entertainment Expenses
Direct Project Costs	Equipment Purchase	For-profit Ventures
Community Engagement	Administrative Overhead	Private Foundations
Educational Initiatives	Training and Workshops	Marketing Campaigns
Capacity Building	Research and Development	Personal Investments
Mission-Related Travel	Technology Upgrades	Religious Activities

Preferred to Fund	May or May Not Fund	Do Not Prefer to Fund
Healthcare Services	Evaluation and Research	Political Advocacy
Youth Development	Scholarships	Animal Testing
Community Development	Outreach and Awareness	International Travel
Environmental Projects	Civic Engagement Projects	Personal Expenses

Budget Justification

The budget justification accompanies the budget section and provides a line-by-line explanation for each budget item. For example, if you have a line item for personnel salaries, the budget justification would explain who these personnel are, their roles in the project, and the basis for their salaries (e.g., industry standards, organization's pay scale). It explains why each expense is necessary for the successful implementation of the project. This may involve discussing how the expense directly supports the project's goals and objectives.

The budget justification outlines the methods used to calculate or estimate costs. For example, if you have travel expenses, you should explain how you arrived at these figures (e.g., airfare, accommodation, per diem rates). It demonstrates the alignment between the budget and the project's activities. The budget justification should highlight how each expense contributes to achieving the project's desired outcomes.

The narrative explains how funding each budget item benefits the grant-making organization (the funder). It might discuss the impact of their support on the organization's mission and the broader community or cause. In some cases, the budget justification might provide a comparative analysis, showing that the proposed costs are reasonable and in line with industry standards or similar projects.

Funders appreciate a transparent and accountable budget justification. It helps build trust and credibility by showing that the organization has thoroughly considered the financial aspects of the project.

The language used in the budget justification should be precise and clear. Avoid jargon and acronyms, and ensure that reviewers can easily understand the justifications. Address potential questions or concerns that funders may have regarding the budget items. Anticipate the kind of information that would reassure them about the responsible use of funds.

Tailor the budget justification to emphasize aspects of the budget that align with the funder's specific priorities and guidelines. This demonstrates that you've customized the proposal to their interests.

In-Kind Contributions in Grant writing

In-kind contributions, often referred to as in-kind donations or non-cash contributions, are a significant aspect of grant writing. In-kind contributions represent the value of goods, services, or resources that are contributed to a project or organization for which no cash is exchanged. These contributions can come from individuals, businesses, or other organizations and are used to support the goals and activities outlined in a grant proposal.

Types of In-Kind Contributions

In-kind contributions can take various forms, including:

- **Goods:** Tangible items such as equipment, supplies, or materials.

- **Services:** Non-cash services provided by volunteers or professionals, such as legal advice, graphic design, or consulting.
- **Facilities:** The use of office space, meeting rooms, or other facilities without charge.
- **Expertise:** Knowledge or skills provided by individuals or organizations, such as training or technical assistance.
- **Volunteer Time:** The value of hours worked by volunteers who contribute their time to support the project.

Valuation

To include in-kind contributions in a grant proposal, it's essential to assign a reasonable and justifiable monetary value to each item or service. Valuation is typically based on market rates, industry standards, or fair market value. For volunteer time, this may be calculated using hourly wage rates for similar work in the local area.

Documenting In-Kind Contributions

It's crucial to maintain records and documentation for in-kind contributions, including descriptions of the items or services, their estimated value, and the sources. This documentation provides evidence to funders of the non-cash support your project is receiving.

Inclusion in the Budget

In-kind contributions are often included in the project budget alongside cash contributions. They increase the overall value of the project without requiring additional cash funding. Funders may view in-kind contributions as a demonstration of community support and as a way to leverage their cash investment.

Narrative Explanation

In your grant proposal, provide a narrative explanation of the in-kind contributions, highlighting how they directly support the project's goals and activities. Explain their relevance and importance to the project's success.

Acknowledgment and Reporting

If awarded the grant, organizations are typically required to acknowledge and report on in-kind contributions throughout the project's duration. This may include documenting volunteer hours, describing how in-kind resources were used, and demonstrating the impact on the project's success.

Compliance with Funder Guidelines

Be sure to review the specific guidelines of the grant-making organization regarding in-kind contributions. Some funders have limitations or specific requirements related to how in-kind contributions are valued and reported.

In-kind contributions are valuable to grant proposals as they help demonstrate the community's commitment to a project and can effectively increase the project's overall budget without requiring additional cash resources. It's essential to accurately value, document, and explain these contributions to present a compelling case to potential funders.

Matching Funds in Grant Writing

Matching funds, also known as cost-sharing or matching grants, are a financial commitment made by a grant applicant or recipient to contribute a specified amount of their own resources or funds to a project. These contributions must be used to match the grant funding being requested from the grant-making organization. Matching funds are a way to leverage grant dollars and demonstrate a commitment to the project's success.

When applying for a grant, the grant-making organization may specify a required match amount or ratio. For example, they might require the applicant to provide a 1:1 match, meaning for every dollar of grant funding requested, the applicant must commit an equal amount from their own resources.

Matching funds can come from various sources, including:

- Cash contributions from the applicant's own funds or revenue.
- In-kind contributions, such as donated goods or services, as discussed in a previous response.
- Third-party contributions from other organizations or partners who are investing in the project.
- Program income generated by the project itself.

Each type of contribution (cash, in-kind, third-party, program income) is typically assigned a specific valuation. Cash contributions are straightforward, while in-kind contributions may require a reasonable and justifiable monetary value. Third-party contributions should be documented and acknowledged by the contributing organization.

The applicant commits to providing the matching funds within the agreed-upon timeframe and ensures they are dedicated to the project's goals. This commitment is a critical part of the grant application and must be fulfilled if the grant is awarded.

Matching funds are often included in the project's budget, demonstrating how they will be used to support the project's activities. Once the grant is awarded, the applicant must report on the use of the matching funds as part of the grant reporting requirements.

Matching funds show the grant-making organization that the applicant is invested in the project's success. It often encourages organizations to secure additional support from other sources, which can significantly increase the project's impact.

Applicants must ensure that they are in compliance with the grant-making organization's guidelines regarding matching funds. This includes accurately valuing, documenting, and reporting on the contributions.

Matching funds are a way for organizations to demonstrate their commitment to a project and to multiply the impact of grant dollars. While they require financial commitment and careful budgeting, they can be a powerful tool in securing and maximizing grant funding. It's essential to be diligent in meeting the matching fund requirements, as failure to do so can jeopardize the grant award.

Evaluation Plan

An evaluation plan in grant writing is a structured framework that outlines how a project or program will be assessed, measured, and analyzed to determine its effectiveness, impact, and alignment with the stated objectives and goals. It encompasses the methods, data collection tools, and evaluation criteria to be used throughout the grant-funded project's lifecycle. It serves as a tool to demonstrate accountability to the grantor, showcasing how funds are being used and how the project is progressing toward its intended outcomes.

An evaluation plan helps assess the project's impact on its target population, community, or cause. It measures the degree to which the project is achieving its goals. It also provides a mechanism for ongoing learning and improvement. By regularly collecting and analyzing data, the organization can make informed decisions to enhance the project's effectiveness.

The Plan fosters transparency by detailing the methods, metrics, and standards used to assess the project. This transparency builds trust with both the funder and the broader community. It addresses the funder's need for evidence of project success and adherence to the grant agreement. A well-executed evaluation plan can lead to increased funder satisfaction and the potential for future funding.

Most times the plan aids in resource allocation by identifying areas of the project that are performing well and those that may need adjustments. This ensures efficient use of resources.

The evaluation plan outlines how findings will be communicated to stakeholders, including the grantor, project staff, and the community. Effective communication supports shared understanding and collaboration. By collecting and analyzing data, the organization can make informed decisions, set priorities, and adjust strategies to achieve the desired outcomes.

Furthermore, an evaluation plan can help identify unintended consequences or side effects of a project, which can inform adjustments and mitigate potential negative impacts. It ensures that the organization complies with reporting requirements stipulated by the grantor, providing data and evidence as requested in the grant agreement.

Tips to Creating an Evaluation Plan

- Choose indicators that are directly linked to the objectives and can accurately measure progress and impact. Indicators should be quantitative or qualitative, depending on the nature of the project.

- Consider a mix of data collection methods, including surveys, interviews, focus groups, observations, and existing records. This provides a more comprehensive view of the project's impact.

- If applicable, collect baseline data before the project begins to establish a starting point for measurement.

- Ensure data quality by using reliable data sources, clear data collection procedures, and well-trained data collectors.

- Develop a clear timeline for data collection, analysis, and reporting. Align this timeline with the project's activities to ensure timely assessment.

- Specify the methods for data analysis. This may include statistical analysis, content analysis, or thematic analysis, depending on the data collected.

- If required, involve external evaluators or consultants with expertise in evaluation and data analysis to ensure quality and impartiality.

- Address ethical considerations in data collection and reporting, including obtaining informed consent from participants, ensuring privacy, and protecting data security.

- Define the format and content of evaluation reports. Tailor reports to the needs of different stakeholders, including the grantor.

- Explain how the evaluation findings will inform decision-making and project adjustments. Demonstrate a commitment to using data for continuous improvement.

- Consider cultural sensitivity in data collection and analysis, ensuring that the evaluation respects and accommodates the diversity of project participants.

- If possible, build the capacity of project staff to participate in the evaluation process. This can foster a culture of learning and improvement.

- Before implementing the evaluation plan, pilot test data collection tools and methods to identify and address any issues or challenges.

- Establish a feedback loop with project staff and stakeholders. This encourages collaboration, ensures that the evaluation stays on track, and addresses any emerging issues.

- Ensure that the budget allocated to the evaluation is adequate to support the planned activities and the quality of data collection and analysis.

- Periodically review and refine the evaluation plan as the project progresses. Flexibility and adaptability are key to maintaining an effective evaluation process.

Here's an example of Evaluation Plan/Metrics for the Non-profit, Girl Child Education.

Project Objectives:

- To increase the enrollment of girls in primary schools by 20% in the first year.

- To improve the overall academic performance of girls, as measured by a 15% increase in the pass rate on standardized tests over three years.

- To enhance girls' life skills and confidence, as evidenced by a 30% increase in self-assessment scores on personal development after two years.

Key Evaluation Elements:

Indicators:

- Indicator 1: Number of enrolled girls in primary schools

- Indicator 2: Pass rate on standardized tests

- Indicator 3: Self-assessment scores on personal development

Data Collection Methods:

- Surveys: Pre-and post-program surveys for participants and parents.
- Interviews: In-depth interviews with participants and key stakeholders.
- Focus Groups: Conduct focus group discussions to gather qualitative insights.
- Observations: Classroom observations and extracurricular activities.
- Existing Records: Review academic records and attendance data.

Baseline Data:

- Collect baseline data on the current enrollment of girls and their academic performance.
- Conduct pre-program surveys and assessments to establish baseline self-assessment scores.

Data Quality:

- Ensure data quality through rigorous training of data collectors.
- Implement consistent data collection procedures and maintain data accuracy.

Timeline:

- Data collection: Conduct baseline data collection in the first quarter of the project.
- Ongoing data collection throughout the project's duration.
- Data analysis: Quarterly analysis with a final comprehensive analysis at the end of the project.

Data Analysis:

- Utilize statistical analysis to measure changes in enrollment and pass rates.
- Conduct thematic analysis of qualitative data to assess personal development.

External Evaluation:

- Engage external evaluators with expertise in education and gender-sensitive evaluations to ensure impartiality and quality.

Ethical Considerations:

- Secure informed consent from participants and parents.
- Protect the privacy of participants and their families.
- Safeguard data security and confidentiality.

Reporting Format:

- Prepare comprehensive reports with both quantitative and qualitative findings.
- Tailor reports for different stakeholders, including the grantor.

Use of Findings:

- Use findings to make informed decisions, adjust program activities, and improve overall project effectiveness.
- Share findings with stakeholders to demonstrate the impact and accountability of the project.

Cultural Sensitivity:

- Ensure data collection and analysis respect the cultural diversity of project participants, recognizing and accommodating cultural differences.

Capacity Building:

- Provide training and capacity building for project staff involved in data collection and analysis to enhance their skills.

Pilot Testing:

- Pilot test data collection tools and methods to identify and address any issues or challenges before full implementation.

Feedback Loop:

- Establish regular feedback loops with project staff and stakeholders to address emerging issues and ensure that the evaluation stays aligned with project goals.

Sustainability Plan

A sustainability plan outlines how an organization intends to continue and maintain the project or program that the grant will fund after the grant period ends. The purpose of a sustainability plan is to demonstrate to grant reviewers that the organization has a long-term strategy for ensuring the ongoing success and impact of the project beyond the initial grant funding.

The sustainability plan shows that the organization has considered how the project will continue to operate and achieve its goals once the grant funding has been expended. This is particularly important for projects that require ongoing resources or support. Organizations should detail how they will secure funding from sources other than the grant, such as through partnerships, fundraising, donations, earned income, or other grants. This diversification of funding sources reduces the project's dependence on a single grant.

The sustainability plan may discuss the commitment of the organization's leadership and stakeholders to support the project or program beyond the grant period. This demonstrates a strong commitment to its success. It can include strategies for engaging the community or target audience to ensure ongoing participation, support, and ownership of the project.

Organizations may describe how they plan to build the capacity of their staff, volunteers, or partners to continue the project successfully. A sustainability plan may address how the project will be continuously evaluated and adapted to remain effective in response to changing needs or circumstances.

It may also outline an exit strategy that explains how the organization would phase out the project if it becomes unsustainable, without causing harm or disruption to the community it serves.

Organizations should discuss how they plan to communicate the project's successes and impact to stakeholders, donors, and the wider community. Regular reporting on progress can help secure future funding and support.

Here's an example of a sustainability plan using our very own Save the Ocean initiative.

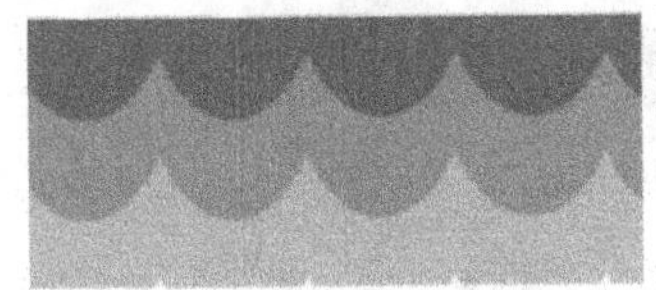

Our mission at "Save the Ocean" is not just about immediate impact; it's about ensuring the longevity of our efforts to protect our oceans. Beyond the grant period, we recognize the importance of diversifying our funding sources. Here's how we plan to ensure the sustainability of our initiatives:

Grant Funding: While we greatly value the grant we've received, we understand the importance of securing additional grant funding. Our dedicated team will continue to search for and apply for grants that align with our goals.

Corporate Partnerships: We will actively seek partnerships with environmentally conscious corporations. These partnerships can include sponsorship deals, cause-related marketing, or collaborative projects that mutually benefit our organization and our partners.

Individual Donations: We will launch targeted fundraising campaigns aimed at individuals who share our passion for ocean conservation. Regular donation drives and donor engagement efforts will be essential to sustaining our work.

Legacy Giving: We will encourage supporters to include "Save the Ocean" in their estate planning and wills. Legacy giving ensures that our cause is supported for generations to come.

Highlighting Partnerships and Collaborations: Collaboration is at the heart of our sustainability plan. We will actively seek partnerships with like-minded organizations, government agencies, and community groups to strengthen our initiatives:

Government Partnerships: We will engage with government agencies and environmental bodies to access additional resources and support for our projects, such as permits, research data, and access to protected marine areas.

Community Alliances: We will foster alliances with local community groups and environmental organizations. These partnerships will enhance our grassroots efforts and promote community ownership of our mission.

Scientific Collaborations: We will establish partnerships with universities and research institutions to advance our scientific understanding of marine ecosystems and to gain access to expert knowledge.

Addressing Risk Factors: We are committed to addressing potential risks and challenges that could affect our project's sustainability. We acknowledge these risks and have strategies in place to mitigate them:

Changing Regulations: We will stay updated with evolving environmental regulations and adapt our projects accordingly to ensure compliance.

Market Volatility: In the face of unpredictable economic conditions, we will diversify our revenue sources to reduce dependency on any single funding stream.

Natural Disasters: As we work in ocean conservation, we are prepared for the impact of natural disasters. We will establish contingency plans to protect our resources and data.

Timeline for Sustainability: We have set a timeline with key milestones to ensure the sustainability of "Save the Ocean":

- Year 1: Secure at least two new grant awards.
- Year 2: Launch a corporate partnership program.
- Year 3: Initiate legacy giving campaigns.
- Year 4: Establish collaborations with government agencies and community groups.

- Year 5: Implement an ongoing research partnership with a local university.

Showcasing Community Engagement: Our community engagement strategy is vital to ensuring long-term support and ownership:

- **Volunteer Programs:** We will expand our volunteer programs, offering opportunities for community members to actively participate in our projects and feel a sense of ownership.
- **Educational Initiatives:** We will create educational programs and workshops for schools and local groups, raising awareness and fostering community involvement.
- **Regular Updates:** We will maintain transparent communication through newsletters and social media, keeping the community informed about our progress and accomplishments.

Performance Metrics and Evaluation: We are committed to tracking our success and impact over time:

- Key metrics include the number of marine species protected, pollution levels reduced, and community involvement levels.
- We will conduct annual performance evaluations and independent audits to ensure accountability and transparency.

Exit Strategy: In the unlikely event that our initiatives become unsustainable, we have a comprehensive exit strategy in place. This involves gradual scaling down, transfer of assets to suitable partners, and transparent communication with stakeholders to ensure minimal harm or disruption.

Supporting Documents

These are an essential part of a grant proposal and provide additional information and evidence to support the main proposal. The specific documents required may vary depending on the grant-making organization and the nature of the project. However, here's a comprehensive list of commonly requested supporting documents when submitting a grant proposal:

Cover Letter: A formal cover letter introducing your organization and the grant proposal.

Executive Summary: A concise summary of the proposal's key points and objectives.

Organizational Information:

- **Mission Statement:** A clear and concise statement of your organization's mission.
- **IRS Determination Letter:** Proof of your organization's tax-exempt status if applicable.
- **Organizational Background:** Information about your organization's history, structure, and leadership.

Project Description:

- **Detailed Proposal:** A comprehensive description of the project or program you're seeking funding for.
- **Program Logic Model or Theory of Change:** A visual representation of how your project will create impact.
- **Needs Assessment:** Data and research supporting the need for the project.
- **Goals and Objectives:** Clear, measurable project goals and objectives.

Budget and Financial Documents:

- **Detailed Budget:** A comprehensive budget for the project, including both income and expenses.
- **Financial Statements:** Current and previous fiscal year financial statements.

- **Audited Financial Statements:** If applicable and available.

Project Timeline: A detailed timeline or work plan outlining the project's milestones and activities.

Evaluation Plan: A plan for how you will measure the success and impact of the project.

Letters of Support: Letters from community partners, stakeholders, or experts endorsing the project.

Resumes and Bios:

- **Key Personnel Resumes:** Resumes of key staff members involved in the project.
- **Board Member Bios:** Biographical information about board members.

Partnership Agreements: Written agreements with collaborating organizations or institutions.

Legal Documents:

- **501(c)(3) Status Documentation:** If applicable.
- **Bylaws:** Your organization's bylaws.
- **Board Meeting Minutes:** Recent minutes from board meetings.

Marketing Materials:

- **Brochures or Pamphlets:** Informational materials about your organization.

- **Website and Social Media Links:** Links to your organization's online presence.

Annual Reports: Recent annual reports highlighting your organization's accomplishments.

Media Clippings: Any press coverage or articles related to your organization or past projects.

Client Testimonials or Success Stories: Personal stories that illustrate the impact of your work.

Environmental Impact Assessment: For projects that may have environmental consequences.

Legal or Regulatory Approvals: Proof of any necessary permits, licenses, or approvals.

Conflict of Interest Policy: Your organization's conflict of interest policy.

Insurance Certificates: Proof of insurance coverage, if required.

Photographs or Visual Aids: Images or visual materials that illustrate the project or organization's work.

Appendices: Any additional documents or information specific to your proposal that aren't covered in the above categories.

How to properly cite your Sources in Grant writing

While writing a statement of need, it is important to include essential data, statistics, analysis, journals, and sources that help to build a case for your proposal. These information shows that there is actually a problem and that this problem is important enough or widespread enough to require an urgent solution. So when you add these statistics or data, you must provide a source to the information given so that the funders can do their due diligence to confirm that what you've written is a fact. Also, it will show that you did some major research adding credibility to your proposal while providing evidence to support your claims. Let's take a look at how to site sources effectively in your grant proposal.

First, you should begin by identifying the source you want to cite. This could be a research study, a government report, a publication, or any source that provides data or information supporting your proposal.

Select an appropriate citation style. Common citation styles in grant writing include APA (American Psychological Association), MLA (Modern Language Association), and Chicago style. Be consistent and use the style required by the grant application guidelines.

If you have done any form of academic writing then you are probably familiar with in-text citations. In-text citations are used within the text of your proposal to acknowledge the source of specific information. These should include the author's last name and the year of publication. If there is no author, use the title of the source. Here's a good example of an in-text citation using APA style:

1. According to Smith (2019), "childhood malnutrition remains a critical issue" (p. 25).
2. "Childhood malnutrition remains a critical issue" (Smith, 2019, p. 25).

Create a reference Section

It is always advisable to include a dedicated "References" section at the end of your proposal. List all the sources you cited in your proposal, following the format required by your chosen citation style. For example, if you are use the APA style of reference then your references will look like this:

Smith, J. (2019). Addressing Childhood Malnutrition: A Comprehensive Study. Publisher.

However, there are various types of formats, depending on whether your source is a book, a journal, a website, a report, or other forms of communication. Let's take a look at some of the differences in how these sources are referenced:

Books follow this format: Author(s). (Year). Title of the book. Publisher.
Example: Smith, J. (2019). Addressing Childhood Malnutrition: A Comprehensive Study. Publisher.

Journal Articles follow this format: Author(s). (Year). Title of the article. Title of the Journal, volume number(issue number), page range.
Example: Brown, L. (2020). The Impact of Education Programs on Child Nutrition. Journal of Public Health, 7(2), 123-136.

Reports follow this format: Author(s). (Year). Title of the report. Publisher.
Example: World Health Organization. (2018). Global Report on Child Nutrition. Author.

Websites follow this format: Author(s). (Year). Title of the web page/document. URL

Example: Centers for Disease Control and Prevention. (2021). Childhood Nutrition Resources. https://www.cdc.gov/nutrition/resources/index.html

When referencing, Double-check the accuracy of your citations to ensure that they match the source material precisely. Verify publication dates, author names, and other details. Consistency is key when citing sources. Use the same citation style throughout your proposal, and follow the specific grant application guidelines for citation formatting.

Properly citing your sources in grant writing not only strengthens your proposal's credibility but also shows respect for the work of others and the importance of accurate information. It is an essential practice for ethical and professional grant writing.

Available on Amazon KDP

Transitioning to
International
Development

The Blueprint to Launching a Career and exploring opportunities in sustainable development.

Brian Obodeze

WRITING A COMPELLING NARRATIVE

Crafting a Powerful Introduction

Crafting a powerful introduction sets the tone for the entire document and captures the reviewer's attention. Here are some professional tips to help you create an impactful and compelling introduction

- Begin with a compelling hook that draws the reader in. This could be a thought-provoking question, a surprising fact, a compelling anecdote, or a powerful quote related to your project or the issue you're addressing.

- In the opening paragraph, clearly and concisely state the problem or need your project aims to address. Provide evidence or data to underscore the significance and urgency of the issue. Make it clear why this problem matters.

- Appeal to the emotions of your readers. Share a relatable story or example that illustrates the human impact of the issue. People often connect more with stories and personal experiences than with statistics alone.

- In the introduction, briefly establish your organization's credibility and expertise in the field. Mention relevant achievements, successful projects, or the qualifications of key team members.

- Offer a glimpse of the solution your project proposes. While you don't need to provide all the details at this point, hint at how your project will make a difference. This should give the reader a sense of hope and optimism.

- Paint a vivid picture of the future you envision. Describe what the world will look like if your project succeeds. Use descriptive and inspiring language to convey your vision.

- Ensure that your introduction explicitly connects your project's goals and the funder's mission or priorities. This demonstrates alignment with their values and increases your chances of success.

- Keep the introduction concise and focused. Avoid unnecessary jargon or technical language. Make every word count.

–   Provide a brief outline of what the reader can expect in the rest of the proposal. This creates a roadmap and helps them navigate the document.

–   Pose questions or tease upcoming information that piques the reader's curiosity, encouraging them to continue reading for answers.

–   Write in the active voice to make your introduction more dynamic and engaging. Active voice sentences are typically clearer and more compelling.

–   Your introduction should be flawless in terms of grammar and punctuation. Errors in the opening section can negatively impact your proposal's credibility.

–   Let your passion for your project shine through in your writing. Authenticity and enthusiasm are contagious and can inspire the reader.

- Don't be afraid to revise your introduction multiple times. The first draft is rarely the best. Keep refining until you achieve a powerful and polished introduction.

- Have others, especially those unfamiliar with the project, read your introduction and provide feedback. This can help you gauge its impact on a broader audience.

Telling your story effectively

Before crafting your story, know your audience, you can do this by researching information on the grant-making organization, its values, priorities, and expectations. Tailor your story to align with their interests. Be sure to focus on the impact of your work as grant reviewers want to know how their funding will make a difference. Share concrete examples of lives changed, communities transformed, or problems solved through previous projects executed by your organization.

Begin your story with a captivating hook, such as a personal anecdote, a relatable problem, or a surprising statistic. This piques the reader's interest from the very beginning. Remember that authenticity is key to effective storytelling so share real stories and experiences that reflect the genuine passion and commitment of your organization as well as unique situations that are based on personal experience.

Use vivid and descriptive language to paint a picture in the reader's mind, this will let them see, feel, and experience your story. Show the impact through sensory details that highlight the human element. Share personal stories of individuals or communities that have benefited from your organization's work or are still benefactors to date. Personal narratives can be more relatable and memorable than general statistics.

Integrate data and facts to reinforce your narrative because numbers can add credibility and context to your story while demonstrating the scale and importance of your work. Organize your story with a clear structure. A typical structure includes an introduction, a compelling main narrative, and a conclusion that ties the story back to the grant proposal's objectives.

Showcase the challenges your organization has faced and how you've overcome them or how they are currently being managed. This demonstrates resilience and adaptability. Also, whenever possible, incorporate visuals like photos, charts, and infographics to complement your story. Visuals can make your narrative more compelling and memorable. Don't forget to incorporate quotes from beneficiaries, volunteers, or community members to provide diverse perspectives and credibility to your story.

Tap into a range of emotions, from empathy and compassion to hope and inspiration. Emotional engagement can leave a lasting impression, but stay focused on the most relevant aspects of your story. Avoid going off on tangents or including unnecessary details.

Finally, conclude your story with a clear call to action that links back to the grant proposal. Explain how the grant funding will help you continue or expand the positive change you've described.

Submission and Follow up

Reviewing Grant Guidelines

Many writers make irreversible mistakes because they do not take the time to go through the grant guidelines. Every grant comes with guidelines on how to write them and how to submit them. So skipping the guidelines means that you expose your organization's proposal to the risk of disqualification. These guidelines are often strict and when something is out of place, it tells the funders that you do not follow instructions or do not consider their need to be important enough. This of course sets the tone. If funders want your fonts to be in Arial, and you submit in Times New Roman, this may be a small oversight that can be overlooked, but because there are thousands of organisations submitting their proposals for funding, this little mistake can be used to screen out proposals that do not follow instructions to the letter. Once you are prepared to write a grant proposal, the first thing to do is to review guidelines. Here are a few things to consider when reviewing grant guidelines.

Obtain the Grant Guidelines: Access the grant guidelines directly from the grantmaker's website or by requesting them from the foundation or organization offering the grant.

Read the Guidelines Carefully: Start by carefully reading through the entire document. Pay attention to details and nuances.

Check Eligibility Requirements: Verify that your nonprofit organization meets all the eligibility criteria, such as nonprofit status, geographic focus, and mission alignment.

Determine Grant Type and Focus: Understand the different grant types offered (e.g., project grants, operational grants) and the specific focus areas or priorities. Ensure your project aligns with these.

Application Deadlines: Note the application deadline and any related dates for notifications and funding disbursement. Create a timeline for proposal development based on this.

Review Application Components: Identify the required components of the grant application. Common components include an executive summary, project description, budget, and supporting documents. Note any specific formats or templates provided.

Evaluation Criteria: Understand how proposals will be evaluated. This may include criteria related to impact, feasibility, innovation, and alignment with the organization's goals.

Budget and Financial Information: Examine the requirements for financial documentation, such as a project budget, audited financial statements, or IRS Form 990.

Reporting and Accountability: Learn about post-award requirements, including reporting schedules and monitoring expectations.

Application Format: Determine the submission format, whether it's through an online portal, email, or physical mail. Ensure you understand the submission process.

Ask Questions and Seek Clarifications: If any part of the guidelines is unclear, reach out to the grantmaker with specific questions or requests for clarification. They often have a contact person for inquiries.

Check for Updates: Ensure that you are working with the most current version of the guidelines, as they can change from year to year.

Post-submission Follow-ups

So you've submitted your grant proposal and your submission was confirmed, now what?

Be Patient: After submitting your proposal, grantmakers often need time to review all applications. Give them the time specified in the grant guidelines before following up.

Record Submission Details: Keep a record of the date and method of submission, as well as any confirmation or acknowledgment of receipt provided by the grantmaker.

Follow Grantmaker's Instructions: Review the grant guidelines for specific instructions on post-submission follow-up. Some grantmakers may prefer certain communication methods or timelines.

Craft a Polite and Professional Email:

- Send a well-crafted, concise follow-up email.
- Express gratitude for the opportunity to apply.
- Mention the title of your proposal and the submission date.

Inquire About the Review Timeline: Ask about the expected timeline for reviewing proposals and when you can anticipate a decision.

Request Confirmation of Receipt: If you didn't receive a confirmation of receipt, politely ask for confirmation that your proposal was received.

Avoid Repetitive Follow-Ups: Don't send multiple follow-up emails in a short span of time. Give the grantmaker ample time to respond.

Include Additional Information Sparingly: If the grantmaker requests additional information or clarification, provide it promptly but concisely. Don't inundate them with unnecessary details.

Stay Professional and Courteous: Maintain a respectful and professional tone in all communication, even if there are delays or setbacks.

Respect the Grantmaker's Response Time: Grantmakers may have specific response times for follow-up inquiries. Wait for their response before sending further follow-up emails.

Seek Feedback (if applicable): If your proposal was declined, politely ask for feedback on why it was not funded. This can provide valuable insights for future applications.

Stay Engaged: Even if you don't receive funding, keep the lines of communication open with the grantmaker. They may have future opportunities or be interested in your organization's progress.

Document All Correspondence: Keep records of all follow-up communication with dates and details. This documentation can be useful for future reference and accountability.

Be Grateful for Any Response: Whether the response is positive or not, express your gratitude for their attention and time.

Learn and Adapt: Use the feedback and insights gained from the post-submission follow-up to improve your future grant proposals. Continuous learning and adaptation are key to success in grant writing.

Handling Rejections and Feedback

Keep in mind that rejections are a part of the grant-seeking process. Approach them with a positive mindset, viewing them as opportunities for growth and learning. It's normal to feel disappointed or discouraged initially. Take time to process your emotions and understand that rejection doesn't reflect your organization's worth. If the grantmaker provides feedback on why your proposal was declined, consider this a valuable opportunity for improvement. Reach out to request feedback if it wasn't provided. Express your gratitude for the feedback you receive, even if it's critical. Acknowledge the effort the grantmaker has put into providing insights.

When you receive feedback, actively listen to the concerns and suggestions provided. Try to understand the grantmaker's perspective. If the feedback is unclear or you need more information to understand the reasons for the rejection, don't hesitate to ask for clarification. Take time to reflect on the feedback and consider how you can use it to improve your future proposals. Identify specific areas for growth and be open to making changes in your proposal, approach, or organization based on the feedback received. Adapt and learn from the experience. As you prepare future grant proposals, implement the lessons learned from the feedback to enhance the quality of your applications.

Even if your proposal is rejected, maintain a positive relationship with the grantmaker. They may have future opportunities that align with your organization's goals. Grant rejections are a part of the process. Embrace resilience and remain committed to your mission and vision. Don't let rejection deter you from seeking other funding opportunities. Keep applying for grants that align with your organization's goals.

Share success stories with funders who have supported your organization. Highlight the positive impact of their funding to reinforce your credibility.

If the grantmaker allows for resubmissions, carefully revise your proposal based on feedback and try again in the future. Remember that the ability to handle rejection and feedback professionally is a valuable skill in the grant writing world. It not only improves your chances of future success but also strengthens your organization's reputation and relationships with grantmakers.

GRANT MANAGEMENT AND REPORTING

Grant Acceptance and Agreements

Grant acceptance is the initial step where the grant recipient formally acknowledges the offer of funding and agrees to the grant's terms and conditions. Here's how it typically works:

After the grantmaker's review process, they will notify the grant recipient of the award. This notification can be in the form of an award letter, an email, or a phone call. The grant recipient is expected to respond to the notification promptly, typically within a specified time frame, to confirm acceptance of the grant. It's important to adhere to the deadline outlined in the notification. Before accepting the grant, carefully review the grant agreement, which is a legally binding document outlining the grant's terms and conditions. Ensure you understand all the requirements and responsibilities. Once you are satisfied with the terms, submit an acceptance letter to the funder, acknowledging your agreement to the grant's terms and conditions. The letter may include details like your organization's name, the grant amount, and the project's title. If there are aspects of the grant agreement that you find challenging to meet, or if you need to make specific changes, communicate with the funder to discuss potential modifications. Be prepared to provide a compelling case for any requested changes.

The grant agreement, on the other hand, is a legally binding contract that spells out the conditions and obligations associated with the grant. It's an important document for both the grant recipient and grantmaker, and it covers several key areas, including:

- **Project Description:** A detailed description of the project or program to be funded, including its goals, objectives, activities, and expected outcomes.
- **Funding Amount:** The specific amount of the grant, including any approved budget modifications.
- **Reporting and Accountability:** Details on reporting requirements, including the frequency, format, and content of reports to be submitted to the funder. This may also include financial reporting.
- **Timeline:** The grant period, including the start and end dates, as well as any milestone deadlines.
- **Use of Funds:** Guidelines on how the grant funds should be used, specifying allowable and unallowable expenses.

- **Compliance:** Requirements related to compliance with laws and regulations, as well as any specific grant-related policies or guidelines.

- **Monitoring and Evaluation:** Details on how the grantmaker will monitor the project's progress and assess its impact.

- **Communication and Public Relations:** Any stipulations related to acknowledging the funder's support and communicating about the project.

- **Financial Reporting:** Requirements for financial reporting, which may include financial statements and documentation of grant fund use.

- **Termination Clause:** Conditions under which the grant agreement may be terminated by either party.

- **Conflict Resolution:** Procedures for resolving disputes that may arise during the course of the grant.

- **Signatures:** Both parties, the grant recipient and the funder, will sign the agreement, indicating their acceptance of the terms and conditions.

- **Legal Counsel:** Depending on the complexity of the grant agreement, it may be advisable to seek legal counsel to ensure your organization's compliance and protection of its interests.

Once the grant agreement is signed by both parties, it becomes a legally binding contract. Both the grant recipient and funders are responsible for adhering to the terms outlined in the agreement throughout the grant period.

It's important to carefully read and understand the terms and conditions, ask for clarification when needed, and fulfill all obligations stipulated in the agreement to ensure a smooth grant implementation process.

Compliance and Reporting Requirements

Every funding agency has their own unique compliance instructions and reporting requirements and these structures are put in place by funders to ensure that the funds are used appropriately, the project is on track, and the goals and objectives are being met. Compliance and reporting are key for accountability and transparency. Here's a few categories under compliance requirements:

Compliance Requirements

Legal and Regulatory Compliance: Nonprofits must comply with all applicable laws and regulations, both at the federal and state levels. This includes ensuring your organization maintains its tax-exempt status, follows accounting standards, and adheres to all relevant nonprofit laws.

Grant Agreement Compliance: The grant agreement, a legally binding document, outlines specific terms and conditions that must be followed. These conditions may include how the grant funds are used, project timelines, reporting requirements, and any other stipulations unique to the grant.

Funding Allocation: Grant funds must be used for the purposes specified in the grant agreement. Any significant deviation from the agreed-upon budget or project scope may require prior approval from the grantmaker.

Financial Recordkeeping: Maintain accurate financial records related to the grant. Grantmakers may require detailed accounting of how funds are spent, and audits might be necessary in some cases.

Financial Reporting: Grant recipients are often required to submit financial reports, such as income statements, balance sheets, or other financial documentation, to demonstrate how the grant funds have been used.

Progress Reports: Regularly provide progress reports to the grantmaker, outlining the achievements and outcomes of the project.

These reports typically include narrative descriptions, data, and measurable indicators.

Audits: Some grants may require financial audits conducted by an independent auditor. The grant agreement or guidelines will specify when and under what circumstances audits are needed.

Compliance with Policies and Guidelines: Adhere to any grantmaker-specific policies and guidelines, such as those related to public relations, branding, or acknowledgment of funding sources.

The non-profit that eventually becomes a benefactor of the grant is obligated to adhere to the terms of compliance as this will breed trust and understanding between the grantor and grantee. Now, let's take a look at the reporting requirements often represented in the agreement.

Reporting Requirements

Frequency of Reports: Grant agreements often stipulate the frequency of required reports. These may be quarterly, semi-annually, or annually, depending on the grant and project timeline.

Content of Reports: The specific content required in reports can vary, but typically includes:

- Progress towards project objectives and goals.

- Financial statements, detailing how grant funds have been spent.

- Information on any challenges or deviations from the original project plan.

- Documentation of any unexpected developments or outcomes.

- Impact assessments, demonstrating the project's effectiveness.

Narrative and Quantitative Data: Reports should combine narrative descriptions of the project's progress and quantitative data to demonstrate the project's impact.

Timely Submission: Submit reports in a timely manner, as specified in the grant agreement. Late or missing reports can result in grant compliance issues.

Request Extensions (if needed): If circumstances prevent you from meeting reporting deadlines, communicate with the funder well in advance to request an extension.

Transparency and Honesty: Be transparent and honest in your reporting, even if the project has faced challenges or obstacles. Transparency builds trust with the grantmaker.

Use of Evidence: Back your reports with evidence, such as data, photographs, testimonials, and other documentation that supports your claims and demonstrates the project's impact.

Prepare for Site Visits: Some grants may include site visits as part of the reporting process. Be prepared to host grantmaker representatives and provide information and updates on the project in person.

Feedback on Reporting: If you receive feedback or requests for additional information from the funder, respond promptly and professionally.

It's essential to stay organized, communicate effectively, and meet all deadlines to fulfill your reporting obligations successfully.

Effective Grant Management Practices

Startups often make the mistake of not taking the time to create a well-rounded grant management structure that gives fluidity to their operations. They may find these structures tedious because of the time and skill required to actually design these structural frameworks, but it does become very necessary along the line. Older non-profits already have systems running for years and when new staff are on boarded, they can easily follow the structures that exist. Here are some practices that startups can adopt as grant management practices.

Thoroughly Understand Grant Requirements: Begin by comprehensively understanding the terms and conditions of the grant, including compliance and reporting requirements.

Establish Clear Roles and Responsibilities: Define roles within your organization for grant management, including who will oversee compliance, financial management, and reporting.

Create a Grant Calendar: Develop a grant calendar that outlines key dates, deadlines, and milestones related to the grant. This helps ensure timely submission of reports and other grant-related tasks.

Develop a Strong Project Management Plan: Create a detailed project plan that outlines project goals, objectives, timelines, and specific activities required to meet the grant's requirements.

Allocate Grant Funds Appropriately: Ensure grant funds are allocated as specified in the grant agreement, and maintain accurate financial records of how the funds are used.

Monitor Project Progress: Regularly track and assess the progress of the funded project, making sure it aligns with the project plan and grant objectives.

Maintain Open Communication: Establish clear communication channels with the grantmaker, and keep them informed of project progress, challenges, and achievements.

Comply with Reporting Requirements: Submit reports on time and in the format specified in the grant agreement. Provide narrative descriptions and quantitative data to demonstrate project impact.

Utilize Evidence and Documentation: Support your reports with evidence, such as data, photographs, testimonials, and other documentation to demonstrate the project's success.

Budget and Financial Management: - Maintain accurate financial records and manage the budget according to the grant's financial requirements. Prepare for potential financial audits.

Seek Legal and Financial Guidance: - Depending on the complexity of the grant and the financial and legal requirements, consider seeking professional guidance from accountants, lawyers, or consultants.

Track In-Kind Contributions: - If your project includes in-kind contributions (non-cash donations), ensure you accurately track and document their value as per grant requirements.

Adjust to Changing Circumstances: - Be flexible and adapt to changes or unforeseen challenges that may arise during the project while keeping the grantmaker informed.

Involve Key Stakeholders: - Engage with key stakeholders, including staff, board members, volunteers, and partners, to ensure everyone is aligned with project goals and grant requirements.

Maintain Clear Records: - Keep meticulous records of all grant-related documents, such as the grant agreement, correspondence, budgets, reports, and receipts.

Use Grant Management Software: - Consider using grant management software or databases to track grant-related tasks, deadlines, and reporting requirements.

Training and Capacity Building: - Invest in training and capacity building for your team to ensure they have the necessary skills and knowledge to manage grants effectively.

Celebrate Achievements: - Recognize and celebrate project milestones and achievements. This not only boosts morale but can also serve as excellent content for reporting.

Plan for Sustainability: - Consider the sustainability of the project beyond the grant period. Develop strategies for continuing the project's impact after the grant concludes.

Develop Long-Term Relationships: - Nurture long-term relationships with funders by demonstrating responsible and impactful grant management, which can lead to future funding opportunities.

Renewals and Extensions

A grant renewal is a process in which a non-profit organization applies for continued funding for a project that has already been funded by the same grantmaker. Renewals typically occur when the initial grant is coming to an end. Non-profits apply for a renewal to continue an existing project that has demonstrated progress and impact. The application process for a renewal may be less extensive than that of a new grant. Non-profits are often required to provide an update on the project's progress, impact, and financial status, along with a request for additional funding. To secure a renewal, non-profits must demonstrate the positive impact of the project, report on any achievements, and provide evidence of how the grant funding contributed to those outcomes. Ensure that the project remains aligned with the grantmaker's goals and priorities, as grant renewals are more likely to be approved when the project continues to meet these criteria.

A grant extension is quite different from a renewal. A grant extension allows non-profit organizations to prolong the duration of a project beyond the initial grant period. This may be necessary when unforeseen circumstances or project delays occur.

Grant extensions are typically requested when a non-profit anticipates that the project won't be completed within the initial grant timeline. Organizations must formally request a grant extension, providing reasons for the extension and a new timeline for project completion. Extensions often require approval from the funder. Non-profits should provide a compelling justification for the extension, explaining the reasons for the delay and outlining how the additional time will ensure the project's success. Grant extensions are subject to approval by the grantmaker. It's important to maintain open communication with the grantmaker to secure their consent for the extension.

Whether applying for a renewal or extension, open and clear communication with the grantmaker is essential. Keep them informed of project progress, challenges, and any need for changes. In both cases, focus on demonstrating the value and impact of the project. Use evidence, data, and outcomes to show how the grant funding has contributed to positive changes. Ensure that renewal or extension requests are submitted well in advance of the grant's end date. It is pertinent to know that late requests may lead to funding gaps.

Furthermore, you should highlight how the project aligns with the grantmaker's goals and mission, emphasizing the importance of continued support. Provide clear financial documentation and reporting to account for the grant funds used during the initial grant period and the additional funding needed for renewals or extensions. Non-profit organizations should be prepared to adapt their projects, timelines, or objectives as needed to accommodate changes during the renewal or extension process.

Grant renewals and extensions provide non-profit organizations with opportunities to maintain and expand projects that are producing positive outcomes or have the potential to create significant positive change over time.

Avoiding Plagiarism and Misrepresentation

If you're using information, data, or ideas from external sources, always provide proper citations. This includes references to research studies, statistics, and any information not generated by your organization. When incorporating content from other sources, use your words to rephrase and summarize the information. This demonstrates your understanding of the material and reduces the risk of unintentional plagiarism. Also, If you want to directly quote a source, use quotation marks and attribute the quote to the original author. Include a proper citation for the source.

Familiarize yourself with the principles of "fair use." While fair use allows for limited use of copyrighted material without permission, it's essential to understand its limitations and to follow copyright laws. Use multiple sources to gather information and support your arguments. This reduces the likelihood of undue reliance on a single source and helps avoid misrepresentation.

When presenting your research data, ensure that it is original and accurate. Manipulating or misrepresenting data is unethical and can damage your organization's credibility. Back up your claims and statements with evidence, such as data, case studies, and testimonials. This strengthens the credibility of your proposal.

After drafting your proposal, thoroughly review and edit the content to ensure that it's free from plagiarism and misrepresentation. Use plagiarism detection tools if necessary. Educate your team members about the importance of avoiding plagiarism and misrepresentation. Provide training on citation, research, and ethical grant writing practices.

Intellectual Property Rights

Intellectual property (IP) rights play a significant role in grant writing, particularly in the context of non-profit organizations seeking funding for projects that involve creative works, innovative technologies, or research. Understanding and addressing IP rights in grant proposals is essential for protecting your organization's interests and ensuring compliance with relevant laws and regulations. There are several types of intellectual property that may come into play when writing a grant proposal:

Copyright: Copyright protects original literary, artistic, and musical works. In grant proposals, this might include written content, images, graphics, or other creative materials.

Trademarks: These protect distinctive symbols, names, and branding. Grant proposals may mention trademarks if they are part of your project's identity or marketing.

Patents: They protect inventions and innovations. If your project involves a new technology or process, it may be subject to patent rights.

Trade Secrets: Trade secrets protect confidential business information, such as formulas, processes, or customer lists. Grant proposals should not inadvertently disclose sensitive trade secrets.

Data and Research: Data and research can also be considered intellectual property. Grant proposals involving data collection or research projects need to address issues of data ownership, access, and sharing.

Ownership and Rights

Grant proposals should clearly specify the ownership and rights associated with any intellectual property involved in the project. If the project uses existing IP, demonstrate that you have the legal rights or licenses to use it.

Licensing and Permissions

If your project involves using copyrighted materials or third-party IP, ensure that you have the necessary licenses or permissions. This should be clearly indicated in the proposal.

Data and Research Ownership

Clearly define who will own and have access to any data or research generated during the project. Grantmakers may want to ensure that data is used for its intended purpose and is not restricted from public benefit.

Phrase Bank for Effective Research Grant Writing

How to put it in Writing

The most challenging aspect of grant writing is finding the right words, terms, and phrases to use when drafting your piece. Most writers encounter this and often find it difficult to maintain tone and language. Transitioning to grant writing can be difficult for those who are not very experienced in mixed forms of writing. In this chapter we will take a look at ways to say what you want to say without sounding informal, inexperienced, or unqualified. Consider this chapter as your phrase bank where you can always return to look up the best ways to describe what you want to say while writing the research part of your grant proposal. So, let's get started.

Introducing a problem

- Addressing a pressing challenge
- Identifying a critical gap
- Confronting a pervasive issue
- Tackling an unmet need
- Responding to an emerging concern

Introducing a problem with time sensitivity

- "Addressing an Imminent Concern"

- "Responding to Time-Sensitive Needs"

- "Urgent Relevance in the Current Climate"

- "Timely Intervention for Impact"

- "Meeting a Time-Critical Challenge"

Establishing importance of topic in recent time

- In recent time, there has been renewed interest in the...

- The last few years have seen a growing trend towards...

- Since it was reported in 2009, XYZ has been attracting considerable interest...

- The past 5 years have witnessed increasingly rapid advances in the field of...

- Recently, developments in the field of XYZ have heightened the need for...

Establishing a controversy within the topic

- To date there is still no agreement on what...

- The concept of XYZ is still under debate...

- Questions have been raised about the use of....

- There are numerous controversies and debates surrounding...

- It still remains in question whether XYZ is ...

Referring to previous work that is already known

- Data from various research studies suggest...
- The existing body of research on XYZ suggests...
- It has been established from a plethora of studies that...
- Several theories on the origin of XYZ have proposed that...
- There is a growing body of literature that recognizes...

Explaining the inadequacies of previous researches

- Previous researches have not dealt with the issue of...
- Most studies in XYZ have failed to address...
- Previous researches are limited to XYZ and only focus on...
- The analysis failed to specify XYZ and also failed to resolve the contradiction between...
- The analysis on XYZ does not take account of ... nor does it examine or take into consideration...

Identifying knowledge gaps

- Little is known about the nature of XYZ...
- The basis of XYZ is poorly understood and there is no data on

  ...

- What is unclear is the future of XYZ and the uncertainty of ...

- The XYZ is still undetermined and no information is available...

Describing your research design and method used

- The study was exploratory and interpretive to determine...
- An empirical research was adopted for this study...
- A holistic approach was utilized, integrating A, B, C to establish...
- The research utilizes a qualitative case study approach to...
- The investigation employs quantitative and qualitative methods in collecting data...

Referencing a previous research

- James's comparative study (2017) found that ...
- Annah's comprehensive review concluded that...
- Chris's (1998) model of XYZ assumes three main...
- Peter's cross-country analysis (2021) showed that...
- Smith's (2020) review of literature concluded that...

Being Cautious when interpreting, explaining, or discussing results

- This rather contradictory result may be due to...
- There are several explanations for this...
- It has commonly be assumed that...
- These findings suggest that...

- The initial observation suggests that there may be a possible link between...
- The data appears to support the assumptions that...
- The evidence clearly suggests
- It implies that a possible implication is...
- These methods are generally known to function...

Advising caution while interpreting results

- This topic must be approached with caution because...
- The findings cannot be extrapolated to suit all patients...
- The results do not rule out the influence of internal factors such as...
- Bear in mind that possible bias exists in these results...
- The data may also be interpreted differently or misconstrued ...

Identifying inadequacies in research

- Previous studies have not dealt with the rising...
- Researchers are yet to treat XYZ in details...
- Most field studies have failed to address...
- Such approaches are limited to local surveys...
- Most of the studies failed to specify.... And shows inconsistencies...

Identifying weaknesses in a research study

- Annah fails to fully define what…
- The author overlooks the distinction between…
- The study appears to be over-ambitious in its claims…
- The author made no attempt to quantify the association between …
- The weakness of the research is the failure to address pre-existing…
- One major drawback of this approach is…
- The limitation of the technique is…
- John's argument relies too heavily on…
- The interpretation overlooks much of historical research

Classifying a subject

- Several taxonomies for XYZ have been developed to…
- Different methods have been proposed to effectively classify…
- There are several categories to distinguish…

Comparative sentences

- In the trial, women were more/less susceptible to the disease than men…
- Women tend to perform better in….

- Women had better affinity for...

- Men had more inclination to XYZ that women

- Men had a more measurable reaction to XYZ compared to women...

Indicating differences across two sentences

- By contrast

- In contrast

- On the other hand

Indicating similarities across two sentences

- Similarly

- Likewise

- In the same way

Introducing meanings

- XYZ can loosely be described as...

- In broad terms, XYZ can be defined as ...

- The term XYZ refers to ...

- The broad use of XYZ is largely equated with...

- The term XYZ connotes...

Demonstrating difficulties in defining a term

- A generally accepted definition for XYZ is lacking…

- A precise definition of XYZ has proved elusive…

- These terms are used interchangeably and without precision…

- XYZ is a rather nebulous term to define…

- There are no specific terms that exclusively define…

Highlighting a trend in a chart, Graph, or table

- What stands out is the rapid increase…

- What is fascinating is the phenomenal growth…

- What is underwhelming is the dramatic decline…

- What can be seen clearly is the dominance…

Describing fractions in statistics

- Over half of those who participated in the survey…

- Nearly half of the respondents(48%) participated…

- Less than a third (32%) of those who took the survey…

- Nearly two-fifth (40%) of married couples attended…

What not to Say When Writing Grant Proposals

When writing grant proposals, it's important to maintain a professional and ethical tone. Avoiding certain phrases and language can help your proposal appear more credible and focused. Here's an extensive list of phrases and words that you should generally avoid in grant proposals:

1. "Guaranteed success"
2. "Free money"
3. "We desperately need funding"
4. "Once-in-a-lifetime opportunity"
5. "Groundbreaking" or "revolutionary"
6. "Secret formula" or "exclusive access"
7. "Cutting-edge technology"
8. "Get rich quick"
9. "Too good to be true"
10. "This will change the world"
11. "Win-win situation"
12. "Limited time offer"
13. "Act now"
14. "Once in a lifetime"
15. "No risk"

16. "Risk-free investment"

17. "This is not a scam"

18. "Cash grant"

19. "As seen on TV"

20. "No strings attached"

21. "Amazing breakthrough"

22. "This is a limited-time opportunity"

23. "Million-dollar opportunity"

24. "New and improved"

25. "Certified"

26. "Money-back guarantee"

27. "You are a winner"

28. "Double your income"

29. "Apply now"

30. "This is a secret"

31. "Join millions"

32. "Get started now"

33. "Congratulations"

34. "The best deal"

35. "Risk-free trial"

36. "One-time investment"

37. "As seen in"

38. "Pre-approved"

39. "Lowest price"

40. "Get out of debt"

41. "Hidden charges"

42. "Earn extra income"

43. "Cure all your problems"

44. "No catch"

45. "Serious cash"

46. "Eliminate bad credit"

47. "Reverses aging"

48. "Do it today"

49. "Satisfaction guaranteed"

50. "No questions asked"

51. "Avoid bankruptcy"

52. "Double your investment"

53. "No credit check"

54. "Save big money"

55. "Get paid"

56. "The following form"

57. "Special promotion"

58. "This isn't a gimmick"

59. "Social Security number"

60. "Great offer"

61. "Hidden assets"

62. "No fees"

63. "This isn't spam"

64. "Congratulations, you're a winner!"

65. "Expect to earn"

66. "Extra income"

67. "Beneficiary"

68. "Astonishing"

69. "Consolidate debt"

70. "Dear friend"

71. "Get it now"

72. "No investment"

73. "Risk-free"

74. "Urgent"

75. "Cash bonus"

76. "Earn $"

77. "Financial freedom"

78. "Great investment"

79. "Home-based"

80. "Multi-level marketing"

81. "Once in a lifetime"

82. "Opportunity"

83. "Promise"

84. "Reserves the right"

85. "This isn't a scam"

86. "We hate spam"

87. "Winner"

88. "Hidden"

89. "Life-changing"

90. "No catch"

91. "This isn't a joke"

92. "Zero percent"

93. "All new"

94. "Bargain"

95. "Cents on the dollar"

96. "Double your"

97. "Explode your business"

98. "Financial freedom"

99. "Free gift"

100. "Income from home"

Avoiding these phrases in your grant proposal will help you maintain a professional, ethical, and credible tone. Funders often look for proposals that present information clearly, honestly, and without the use of hyperbolic or misleading language.

Grant writing innovation for the future

The future of grant writing is evolving in response to changes in technology, society, and the philanthropic landscape. While the core principles of effective grant writing remain constant, several trends and developments are shaping its future.

Grant writers are increasingly using technology and software tools to streamline the grant application process. Automation and AI-driven systems can help in researching grants, drafting proposals, and tracking progress. This can save time and reduce the administrative burden, allowing grant writers to focus on strategy and storytelling

The importance of data in grant proposals is growing. Funders are looking for evidence-based programs and measurable outcomes. Grant writers must be proficient in data collection, analysis, and impact assessment to create persuasive proposals

Funders are often looking for collaborative efforts and multi-stakeholder partnerships. Grant writers must understand how to navigate and negotiate these complex relationships and convey them effectively in proposals.

The rise of remote work, as seen in many industries, has also affected grant writing. Grant writers can work for organizations worldwide, expanding opportunities and collaborations across borders.

Grant proposals are increasingly expected to address diversity, equity, and inclusion. Grant writers must demonstrate a commitment to these principles and incorporate them into program design and reporting.

Many funders are moving their application processes to online platforms, making it essential for grant writers to be adept at navigating these systems. Learning the ins and outs of various platforms will become a crucial skill.

Funders are looking for projects that have sustainable, long-term impacts. Grant writers will need to emphasize the long-term viability and scalability of programs in their proposals.

Effective storytelling remains paramount. Grant writers must be skilled in creating compelling narratives that resonate with funders and convey the human impact of their projects.

Ethical considerations in grant writing are increasingly important. Grant writers must maintain transparency, avoid plagiarism, and uphold the highest ethical standards to build trust with funders.

As funders demand greater accountability, the ability to effectively monitor and report on grant-funded projects will become even more critical. Grant writers need to be skilled in this area to fulfill reporting requirements.

Grant writing has been influenced by the COVID-19 pandemic, as funders have shifted priorities to address immediate needs. Flexibility and the ability to respond to crisis situations will continue to be relevant.

The field of grant writing is seeing increased educational opportunities, including formal degree programs and online courses. This growth in education will likely lead to more skilled grant writers in the future.

The urgency of addressing climate change and environmental issues is influencing grant funding. Grant writers who can articulate projects related to environmental sustainability may find new opportunities.

In conclusion, the future of grant writing is marked by both continuity and adaptation. While the fundamentals of effective grant writing will persist, the evolving landscape demands that grant writers embrace technological advancements, data-driven approaches, ethical practices, and a deep understanding of the specific needs and priorities of funders. The role of grant writers is more vital than ever in securing resources for projects that address critical issues and contribute to positive social change on a local, national, and global scale.

Professional tools for conducting data-driven research in the field of Grant writing

Data.gov: Data.gov is a comprehensive resource that provides access to a vast array of datasets from the U.S. government. It covers a wide range of topics, making it a valuable source for grant writers, particularly for projects in the United States.

Google Scholar: Google Scholar is a free search engine that focuses on academic and scholarly sources. It's a valuable tool for finding research articles, papers, and publications related to your grant proposal.

Census Bureau Data Tools: The U.S. Census Bureau offers a variety of data tools and resources, including the American FactFinder and

Data.census.gov, which provide demographic and economic data that can support grant proposals.

Statista: Statista is a leading source of statistical information and data visualization. It offers access to a wide range of data across numerous industries and sectors.

World Bank Data: The World Bank provides an extensive collection of data on global development. It offers valuable information for international grant proposals related to economic development, poverty reduction, and more.

OpenRefine: OpenRefine is a free, open-source tool that helps clean and transform messy data. It's useful for preparing data for analysis and ensuring data quality.

Tableau Public: Tableau Public is a powerful data visualization tool that allows you to create interactive and shareable data visualizations. It's particularly useful for presenting data in a compelling way.

SPSS (Statistical Package for the Social Sciences): SPSS is a widely used statistical software program that is helpful for in-depth data analysis. It can be useful for grant writers who need to conduct advanced statistical analyses.

NVivo: NVivo is a qualitative data analysis software that can be beneficial for projects involving in-depth qualitative research. It helps with coding, analyzing, and visualizing unstructured data.

Excel and Google Sheets: These spreadsheet tools are essential for organizing and analyzing data. They are widely accessible and offer basic data analysis capabilities.

SurveyMonkey: If your research involves surveys, SurveyMonkey is a popular tool for creating, distributing, and analyzing survey data.

Qualtrics: Qualtrics is a comprehensive online survey platform that provides advanced survey design and data analysis features.

EndNote or Zotero: These reference management tools help you manage and cite the sources you use in your grant proposal. They can be particularly useful when conducting extensive literature reviews.

SAS (Statistical Analysis System): SAS is a robust statistical software suite commonly used for advanced data analysis and reporting. It's suitable for complex data-driven research.

Power BI: Microsoft's Power BI is a data visualization and business intelligence tool that can help you create interactive and insightful data reports and dashboards.

QGIS: QGIS is an open-source geographic information system (GIS) software that can be used for spatial data analysis and mapping in grant proposals that involve geospatial data.

R: R is an open-source programming language and software environment for statistical computing and graphics. It's highly versatile and often used for complex data analysis.

Stata: Stata is a statistical software package that's widely used for data analysis and visualization. It's popular in both academic and research settings.

Mendeley: Mendeley is a reference manager and academic social network that helps with organizing and citing research materials.

PubMed: PubMed is a free database of biomedical literature. It's an excellent resource for health and medical-related grant proposals.

Web of Science: Web of Science is a multidisciplinary citation database that can help you discover research articles and track citations.

ProQuest: ProQuest is a database of academic theses, dissertations, and research reports. It's a valuable resource for comprehensive literature reviews.

Datawrapper: Datawrapper is an online tool for creating interactive data visualizations and charts. It's user-friendly and doesn't require coding skills.

Epi Info: Epi Info is a free tool for epidemiology and public health research. It can assist in data management and basic analysis.

Socrata: Socrata is a cloud-based platform for data analysis and visualization, often used by government agencies and organizations for sharing data.

Atlas.ti: Atlas.ti is qualitative data analysis software that helps researchers manage and analyze unstructured text and multimedia data.

MAXQDA: MAXQDA is another qualitative data analysis software with a focus on text analysis, coding, and visualization.

Google Trends: Google Trends provides insights into search trends over time. It can be valuable for demonstrating the interest or relevance of your project.

PolicyMap: PolicyMap is an online mapping tool that provides access to a wealth of data, including demographics, housing, and more.

Sway: Microsoft Sway is a presentation tool that can help you create interactive, visually engaging reports and proposals.

QlikView: QlikView is a business intelligence platform that offers data visualization and analytics capabilities for grant reporting.

IBM SPSS Statistics: IBM SPSS is a widely used statistical software for data analysis, including advanced statistical tests.

SurveyGizmo: SurveyGizmo is a robust survey and data collection platform that offers in-depth reporting and analysis features.

D3.js: This is a JavaScript library for creating interactive data visualizations on the web. It's highly customizable and suitable for web-based proposals.

Qualrus: Qualrus is qualitative data analysis software that provides tools for coding, text analysis, and concept mapping.

SIFT (Social Impact and Financial Transparency): SIFT is a platform for nonprofit organizations to manage, analyze, and report their financial and impact data.

JMP: JMP is a data analysis and visualization tool often used in scientific research and data-driven decision-making.

SciVal: SciVal is a research performance evaluation tool that can assist in gathering data to support the importance of your project.

QDA Miner: QDA Miner is qualitative data analysis software that aids in text analysis, content coding, and data management.

ResearchGate: ResearchGate is a platform for researchers to discover and access academic publications and collaborate with peers.

EconData: EconData is a resource for economic data, statistics, and time series information that can be valuable for economic and social science research.

SageMaker: Amazon SageMaker is a cloud-based platform for machine learning and data science, which can be useful for predictive analytics in grant proposals.

Quantrix: Quantrix is a modeling and data analytics tool that can help with financial planning and forecasting in grant applications.

Wolfram Alpha: Wolfram Alpha is a computational search engine that can provide answers to factual and data-driven questions.

Trello: Trello is a project management tool that can help you stay organized and manage your grant proposal process, including data collection and analysis.

Camtasia: Camtasia is a video editing and screen recording tool that can be useful for creating multimedia content to enhance grant proposals.

IdeaScale: IdeaScale is an innovation management platform that can help you gather data and feedback for innovation-focused grant proposals.

Lucidchart: Lucidchart is a diagramming and visualization tool that can help create flowcharts, process maps, and diagrams for your proposal.

QuickBooks: QuickBooks is accounting software that can assist in managing grant finances and budget reporting.

Geospatial Data Portals: Various geospatial data portals, such as Data.gov's geospatial resources or the Global Forest Watch, provide geospatial data for environmental and spatial analysis.

Crimson Hexagon: Crimson Hexagon is a social media analysis tool that can help analyze social media data for insights related to your grant proposal.

ArcGIS: ArcGIS is a comprehensive geospatial software for mapping, spatial analysis, and data visualization.

Pollfish: Pollfish is a mobile survey platform that can be used for conducting surveys and gathering data from mobile users.

Bioinformatics Tools: If your grant proposal is related to life sciences or genomics, tools like BLAST, NCBI, and Galaxy Project can be valuable for data analysis.

Salesforce Nonprofit Success Pack: If you're working with a nonprofit organization, Salesforce NPSP offers tools for data management and donor relationship tracking.

ePACT Network: ePACT is a network for emergency data and communication that can be valuable in emergency response and community-based grant proposals.

EpiCollect: EpiCollect is a free app and web tool for mobile data collection that's useful for field research and data gathering.

Zoho Analytics: Zoho Analytics is a business intelligence and data analytics platform that can help you analyze and visualize data for grant proposals.

Quillbot: Quillbot is an AI-powered writing and editing tool that can help refine the language and clarity of your grant proposal.

Matomo: Matomo is an open-source web analytics platform that can help you track website data and user behavior for web-based projects.

Looker: Looker is a business intelligence and data analytics platform that enables organizations to explore, analyze, and share data insights.

Crimson Hexagon: Crimson Hexagon, now known as Brandwatch Consumer Research, is a social listening and consumer insights platform that can provide valuable data on consumer sentiment and trends.

Sigma Computing: Sigma is a cloud-based business intelligence and data analytics tool that allows users to perform data analysis and visualization in a collaborative environment.

Visage: Visage is a data visualization tool that focuses on creating custom infographics and data-driven visuals for reports and presentations.

Bloomberg Terminal: For financial or economic research, the Bloomberg Terminal provides real-time market data, news, and analytics.

RapidMiner: RapidMiner is a data science platform that offers a range of data analysis and machine learning tools for predictive analytics.

OnTheMap: OnTheMap is a web-based mapping and reporting tool that provides access to a wide range of employment and workforce data.

SimplyAnalytics: SimplyAnalytics is a web-based mapping and data visualization tool that can help you analyze demographic and market data for grant proposals.

Datawrapper: Datawrapper is an online tool for creating data visualizations, charts, and maps to present your data effectively.

SAS Visual Analytics: SAS Visual Analytics is a data visualization and business intelligence tool for exploring and sharing insights from your data.

Google Analytics: Google Analytics helps you track website and online campaign performance, which can be valuable for grant proposals involving online outreach and impact.

Pew Research Center: The Pew Research Center offers a wealth of data and reports on various topics, including social trends and public opinion, which can support your research.

NIH RePORTER: The National Institutes of Health (NIH) RePORTER provides access to research projects and funding data, making it essential for health-related grant proposals.

Want More Great Books from the Author?

Check out these awesome reads

ADVANCED
UX
WRITING
BEST PRACTICES FOR ENGAGEMENT,
COMPETITION, AND CONVERSION.
BRIAN
OBODEZE

LAW
of
CONTRACTS
for
BUSINESS
Mastering Contract Law
Maximizing Business Opportunities and
Minimizing Legal Risks
Brian Obodeze

GRANT
Vocabulary
and
Terminologies
for Advanced
Wordsmiths.
Practical Grant writing
keywords, phrases,
terms, and definitions
simplified for
effective writing.
WRITING
Brian Obodeze